PRAISE FOR *WOMEN LIVING WELL*

Each day, as Christian wives and mothers, we fight the urge to take in the forbidden fruit of this world. Courtney's grasp on biblical truth and encouragement to "love living it out" is unlike anyone's I've ever met.

—Janelle Nehrenz, blogger, Comfy in
the Kitchen; contributor to *Women
Living Well*

Women Living Well is an eloquent and inspiring book full of practical encouragement as well as tangible steps we can all take to bring our walk closer to the Lord. Courtney addresses struggles that every woman faces and provides wonderful insight into how we can fully redeem the precious time we have with our Lord, our families, and our roles as Christian women living in today's world.

—Erica Arndt, author; blogger,
Confessions of a Homeschooler

Powerful, inspiring, captivating. Courtney clearly calls women to live their lives with intentionality and provides sound direction and motivating encouragement to those who long to live confidently for God's purposes. This book is a must-read for those wanting to lead a powerful and meaningful life.

—Sally Clarkson, author, *Desperate*

I love Courtney's balanced biblical approach to women living well. Her thoughts are sincere, her voice beautifully endearing, and her ideas refreshingly helpful. And as always, she keeps her perspectives coming from a heart totally sold out to Jesus.

—Lysa TerKeurst, *New York Times*
best-selling author, *Unglued*; president,
Proverbs 31 Ministries

Women Living Well is a grace-filled roadmap for biblical womanhood in today's culture. Using Scripture and real-life examples, Courtney gives us practical instruction on how to live for God while serving as a homemaker, wife, and mother—and proves it's not only possible but fulfilling too! Her passion for the Lord is contagious and shines through every word she writes. If there's one book to read this year on serving Jesus as a modern woman, this is it.

—Mandy Ballard, conference speaker;
blogger, BiblicalHomemaking.com

Courtney Joseph delivers a hard-to-put-down book that I have been extremely blessed by. I would highly recommend *Women Living Well* as a biblical resource that all women looking to grow in their walk with the Lord should read.

—Kylie Bisutti, author, *I'm No Angel*

Here is what I love about Courtney Joseph—and why I believe you will love this book—she lives the life she writes about. So often those in ministry say one thing publicly and live a very different life privately. Courtney loves and respects her husband, she bows down before the King in her daily walk, and she builds women up by encouraging them to do the same.

—Fawn Weaver, author, *The Happy Wives Club*

Every woman needs to read this book to help her draw from the living well.

—Janice Le, founder, Women After God and Encouragement Through Biblical Words

This book is full of timeless truths that will lead women to a more joy-filled life. In an increasingly busy world, Courtney inspires us to slow down and get a proper perspective of what matters most.

—Candace Cameron Bure, actress, author, speaker

In a culture that offers fast fixes and snazzy shortcuts that promise to lead women to happiness but rarely ever satisfy, Courtney Joseph's *Women Living Well* offers the truth: we as women can only live well when we intentionally drink deep from the true wellspring of life—Jesus Himself. This volume is chock-full of biblical advice and practical inspiration that will help you to effectively live and love God, your husband, your kids, and your home—in that order.

—Karen Ehman, Proverbs 31 Ministries, Director of Speakers; author, *LET. IT. GO*; wife of Todd and mother of three

Women Living Well is a rare gem in this modern world, and a must-have companion for women. Courtney's Christ-centered approach to life is right on the mark cheering us on to the finish line. With wisdom and guidance, she encourages us to grab hold of God and dig into His Word. This book left me feeling challenged, refreshed, and inspired!

—Darlene Schacht, author, *The Time-Warp Wife*, www.timewarpwife.com

Women Living Well is a beautifully written, warm, wise, and very practical guide for wives. And, it's based on the Bible. Courtney Joseph is refreshingly honest and real. She knows how to live well and she can show you how.

—Dr. David Clarke, Christian psychologist; speaker; author, *Married but Lonely* and *Kiss Me Like You Mean It*

Women Living Well is a MUST read for all women! With an organized, comprehensive, and real-life approach Courtney Joseph reaches the hearts of women across the world. As you follow along with Courtney's candid journey, you will find yourself inspired and challenged to live this one life well.

—Ruth Schwenk, www.thebettermom.com

Does motherhood have to be an endless, chaotic, exhausting guilt trip? Courtney Joseph doesn't think so! In this practical, inspiring book, she shows women there's an alternative to the frantic "keeping up with the Joneses" modern mentality. It is possible to live well in the modern world--by traveling backward in time to the Savior who beckons us toward peace, purpose, and powerful parenting.

—Sheila Wray Gregoire, blogger, ToLoveHonorandVacuum.com.

Women Living Well is the perfect title for this book as it does indeed demonstrate how we can all live well in our lives!

—Clare Smith, www.peak313.com

I have had the honor of being best friends with Courtney since we were carefree teenagers in high school, laughing at ourselves and dreaming of what God might have in store for our lives. Though Courtney and I have evolved over the years from teenagers to wives and mothers, one thing which hasn't changed is Courtney's passion and love for God. I know I wouldn't be the same person without her influence in my life, and after reading her book, I dare to say the same will be true for you! *Women Living Well* is a modern day guide designed to help our generation learn to "Walk with the King" in all areas of our lives.

—Angela Perritt, cofounder, GoodMorningGirls.Org

With her warm, inviting style I feel as if Courtney has become a close and caring friend through these pages, but mostly I feel more connected to Jesus, my close and caring Friend, who is always there for me, even in my busy life. I highly recommend this book!

—Tricia Goyer, author, *One Year of Amish Peace*

Women Living Well gives a practical and applicable guide to help women as they seek to be Godly mothers and wives. We need more of these values in our homes today and I'm thankful for Courtney's heart and the mission God has given her.

—Kelly Stamps, author, Kellyskornerblog.com

I long to live well and love well, yet many days I feel pulled from every direction, divided into a million pieces, and left with so little to give to those I love. If that's you too, pull up a chair and spend time with my friend, Courtney Joseph. In *Women Living Well*, she offers an inspirational and practical road map for today's busy Christian woman who wants God's best for her marriage, her parenting, her homemaking, and her everyday life. This is a book I'll read again and again.

—Renee Swope, Proverbs 31 Ministries radio cohost; speaker; best-selling author, *A Confident Heart;* www.ReneeSwope.com

I was inspired reading *Women Living Well*. This is the story of every woman's desires--to live well. Courtney's personal example of finding joy in every area of her life inspires me daily and her book is the heartbeat of our every day lives.

—September McCarthy, author, *One September Day*

WOMEN
LIVING WELL

WOMEN LIVING WELL

Finding Your Joy in God,
Your Man, Your Kids, and Your Home

COURTNEY JOSEPH

NELSON
BOOKS

An Imprint of Thomas Nelson

Published in Nashville, Tennessee, by Nelson Books, an imprint of Thomas Nelson. Nelson Books and Thomas Nelson are registered trademarks of HarperCollins Christian Publishing, Inc.

Thomas Nelson, Inc., titles may be purchased in bulk for educational, business, fund-raising, or sales promotional use. For information, please e-mail SpecialMarkets@ThomasNelson.com.

Published in association with Esther Fedorkevich, The Fedd Agency, Austin, TX.

Unless otherwise noted, Scripture quotations are taken from THE ENGLISH STANDARD VERSION. © 2001 by Crossway Bibles, a division of Good News Publishers.

Scripture quotations marked NIV are taken from the Holy Bible, New International Version®, NIV®. Copyright © 1973, 1978, 1984, 2011 by Biblica, Inc.™ Used by permission of Zondervan. All rights reserved worldwide. www .zondervan.com

Italics added to Scripture quotations are the author's own emphasis.

The websites recommended in this book are intended as resources for the reader. These websites are not intended in any way to be or to imply an endorsement on behalf of Thomas Nelson, nor does the publisher vouch for their content for the life of this book.

Library of Congress Cataloging-in-Publication Data

Joseph, Courtney, 1975–
  Women living well : finding your joy in God, your husband, your kids, and your home / Courtney Joseph.
    pages cm
  Includes bibliographical references and index.
  ISBN 978-1-4002-0494-6 (alk. paper)
  1. Christian women—Religious life. I. Title.
  BV4527.J69 2013
  248.8'43—dc23   2013007931

Printed in the United States of America

13 14 15 16 17 QG 6 5 4 3 2 1

To my mom—
*I am forever grateful that you led me to the living
well and showed me how to walk with the King.*
I love you.

Her children rise up and call her blessed.
—Proverbs 31:28

❦

To my dad—
*Your faithfulness to God and to your family has been a
source of comfort, security, and courage to me. Thank you for
displaying the love of our heavenly Father as my earthly father.*
I love you.

*One generation shall commend your works to another,
and shall declare your mighty acts.*
—Psalm 145:4

CONTENTS

CONTENTS

WHICH VOICE ARE
YOU LISTENING TO?

V oices.

Voices. They come at us from every side.
We listen to the voices on the iPad. The iPod. The iPhone.
But are we listening to the voice of the Great I AM?

> *The voice of the LORD* is over the waters;
> the God of glory thunders,
> the LORD, over many waters.
> *The voice of the LORD* is powerful;

the voice of the LORD *is full of majesty.*
The voice of the LORD *breaks the cedars;*
the LORD breaks the cedars of Lebanon.
He makes Lebanon to skip like a calf,
and Sirion like a young wild ox.
The voice of the LORD *flashes forth flames of fire.*
The voice of the LORD *shakes the wilderness;*
the LORD shakes the wilderness of Kadesh.
The voice of the LORD *makes the deer give birth*
and strips the forests bare,
and in his temple all cry, "Glory!"
The LORD sits enthroned over the flood;
the LORD sits enthroned as king forever.
May the LORD give strength to his people!
May the LORD bless his people with peace!
(Ps. 29:3–11)

The voice of the Lord is powerful and majestic, yet it is nearly impossible to hear over the clamor of this world. Will you join me on a journey to be women living well as we intentionally block out the world's noise and tune in to the voice of our Creator? He loves us, and He longs to speak to us.

Be still and listen with me.

Come.

Let's walk with the King.

Part 1

YOUR WALK
WITH THE KING

*For my people have committed two evils: they have forsaken
me, the fountain of living waters, and hewed out cisterns
for themselves, broken cisterns that can hold no water.*

—JEREMIAH 2:13

L iving well in this modern world is a challenge. Increased responsibilities, kids' activities, and the new front porch of social media have changed the landscape of our lives. Women have been told for far too long that being on the go and accumulating more things will make our lives full. As a result we grasp for the wrong things in life and come up empty.

God created us to walk with Him, to know Him, and to be loved by Him. He is our living well, and when we drink from the water He continually provides, His living water will change us, making us more like Jesus.

1

I WANT THE SPA, BUT
I NEED SOLITUDE
WITH GOD

*God pictures himself as a mountain spring of clean, cool,
life-giving water. The way to glorify a fountain like this is
to enjoy the water, and praise the water, and keep coming
back to the water, and point other people to the water,
and get strength for love from the water, and never, never,
never prefer any drink in the world over this water.*

—JOHN PIPER, *WHEN I DON'T DESIRE GOD*

I pulled back the curtain to unveil the breathtaking landscape
of New York City. As I peered out the window from my thirty-
seventh-floor hotel room, I had flashbacks of Chicago. Fifteen years
earlier I had lived in that city while attending Moody Bible Institute.
Many times I had looked out the window at the urban landscape of
that Midwestern metropolis and prayed, "God, use me."

As a teenager, I dreamed of becoming a missionary, of taking
the love of Jesus somewhere on the other side of the globe. However,
upon graduation from college I married my high school sweetheart
and moved back home to Ohio.

For years I led women's Bible studies, retreats, and workshops, until one day I decided to move my ministry online by starting a blog. Before long, receiving e-mails from ladies in Egypt, Croatia, Germany, Brazil, or Japan became the norm. I was reaching the other side of the globe as I'd hoped, but instead of dwelling in a foreign land, I was doing it from my kitchen computer. God had truly given me the desires of my heart!

As I stood in New York City, looking out my hotel room, I realized I was having a full-circle moment. My prayer had not changed. Soon to appear with my husband before thousands of television viewers, I gathered my courage and whispered again, "God, use me."

An hour later, I was in the green room, getting stage makeup and being drilled with questions by producers to prepare Keith and me for our interview with the nationally syndicated, daytime talk show host Rachael Ray. I clenched my husband's hand tightly as the cameras began to roll.

Five days earlier, cameras had invaded our home, catching me doing what I do best and most—cooking, cleaning, and taking care of my husband and children. It sure didn't feel television-worthy, but to Rachael Ray my lifestyle was an anomaly! She placed the title on me of "Time-Warp Wife," and Keith and I proceeded into our interview.

Right out of the gate Rachael asked, "Is this always the way you envisioned your life growing up?"

I answered with a nervous smile. "Yes, I went to college. I graduated with honors. I could have chosen to have a career, but once I married my husband, *he* became my career. I love taking care of him. I find fulfillment in that."

Rachael replied, "So this works for you. It was a conscious choice."

I answered, "It's hard work to take care of the home. It is a job, and I do it full-time."

A minute later Rachael called out to the audience, "Show of hands. Is there anyone here who finds this a little offensive?"

There was a pause as the audience responded with a raise of hands.

Voices. These are the voices to which I choose not to listen. They don't have the right to speak into my life.

Rachael went on, seeming slightly baffled that I would choose to live this way. "It's a different concept. Now, do you actually schedule time for yourself each day? Because I think that's something every woman should do."

"Oh yes!" I replied. "I think women need to get their rest. We need to take care of ourselves emotionally, physically, spiritually . . ."

Cut! When the show aired, the word "spiritually" was edited out.

I went on, "We need to take care of ourselves so we have more to give."

Rachael interrupted, "You literally schedule some time for yourself each day?"

"Yes, every evening I head to the treadmill, and in the morning I have a quiet time where I meet with God to prepare for my day."

Cut! When the show aired, they ended the sentence after I said "quiet time."

My walk with God was literally edited right out of my life.

What viewers saw on the show that day was not the full story. If only I could have explained more—more about my climb, more about the journey through dark valleys, through green pastures, beside quiet waters. If only viewers could have heard about the Shepherd who has been with me every step of the way, how His rod and staff have comforted me.

There I sat on the mountaintop—in the national spotlight—but the audience had no desire to hear about the long climb that had brought me there.

Walk with the King

In 2010, I spoke at a bloggers' conference. After one of the sessions, a girl sat down beside me. She told me she noticed that I sign every blog post "Walk with the King." Then she explained that she prefers to refer to her walk with God as a hike.

Yes—a hike! My walk with God often feels more like a hike than a leisurely stroll. I have hiked with God through many seasons of life: attending public school, falling in love, going to college, getting married, having children, choosing homeschooling, and now leading an online ministry. Along the way, I have encountered both valleys of despair and mountaintop experiences.

One biblical role model I've studied along my trek is a man who is mentioned just a few times in the Bible, yet he had the ultimate hike—all the way to heaven! His name was Enoch.

In Hebrew, the name Enoch means "dedicated," or "devoted." Genesis 5:24 tells us, "Enoch walked with God, and he was not, for God took him." Hebrews 11:5 further explains, "By faith Enoch was taken up so that he should not see death, and he was not found, because God had taken him. Now before he was taken he was commended as having pleased God."

Enoch walked with God, and God was so pleased with His hiking companion that He took him off planet Earth to be with Him in heaven. Can you imagine? I marvel at this! How in the world did Enoch "walk with God"? I want to walk with God like that! Clearly, Enoch lived out the fullness of his name: he was *devoted* to God.

SLOW DOWN TO CONNECT WITH GOD

Have you ever thought about why we call our daily Bible readings *devotions*? I've heard people say, "The words *quiet time* and *devotions* are not in the Bible, so meeting with God daily is optional." Indeed they are correct. God does not command us in Scripture to have a set time to meet alone with Him each day. Walking with God means we live every minute devoted to God. This is a challenge in our fast-paced world.

Electricity has created an artificial day during our nights. Rather than sleeping like most of nature does, when the sun goes down we try to defy nature and keep going as if it is still daytime. We live in a world that runs 24/7. Computers, televisions, cell phones, the Internet, restaurants, grocery stores, and more are at our access around the clock. We try to keep pace with our hyperactive culture, and then we wonder why we, and some of our children, are so . . . well . . . hyperactive!

We must slow down and create calm moments. It is in our unhurried moments that we can see and hear clearly.

When we are on the go-go-go, we can't see the person who is hurting and needs a hug. We can't perceive our husbands' need for our tender affection. We don't have time to linger at the bedsides of our children to really listen. We don't write an encouraging note to a friend who is hurting. We can't enjoy the sunrise, a surprise game of hide-and-seek, or a spontaneous song of praise. And we certainly cannot hear God's voice clearly.

It is in our slow moments when we best connect with our Creator.

We women carry a long to-do list and heavy burdens. Consider Jesus for a moment. He carried with Him the burdens of the entire world. He knew every hurt and pain each man, woman, and child faced. The needs He was aware of were beyond what we can understand, yet He did not help everyone. He did not hurry in a speed of flurry to complete as much as He could before sunset. He took time along the way to stop and talk to people. Early in the morning He made time to be alone with His Father, the King. He even rested while a raging storm brewed all around Him at sea (Matt. 8:23–24).

Sweet reader, when we do not slow down and rest, we miss God's voice. We tend to feel overwhelmed, irritable, frustrated, and unappreciated. Emotionally we can lose our way. We have been deceived into thinking that more is better: more food, more clothes, more toys, and more decorations. "More, more, more" falsely promises to make us happy. Even when we are pursuing something noble, such as serving others or volunteering, the overactivity threatens to bring chaos to our homes and families.

This frantic pace most often means that we are also lacking in time alone with God to listen, gain strength, and glean wisdom. Sadly, we begin to act like the rest of the world, grasping for joy in things and activity. Eventually, we find a slow moment—but rather than hearing God's voice, we only hear the voice of guilt beckoning us to get moving again.

Maybe the solution is a spa day—a day away from the hustle and bustle to just relax and refresh. While I think spa days are a wonderful treat, I believe that what we need even more as women is solitude with Jesus. Solitude is powerful. Solitude brings perspective. And sadly, solitude is something most of us rarely get.

In the part of my life I like to call B.C. (before children), it was not difficult to find moments of solitude. Once I brought my first baby home from the hospital, however, my life was forever changed! I remember taking a shower with the bouncy seat right outside the shower curtain. I'd peek out to check on my little boy, and there he was sitting, happy as a lark, delighted by the sound of the water. He may have been content and cooing, but I was whining because my solitude was now gone!

As the children grew, so did their tactics to sabotage my solitude. We lived in an older home, where the floors were uneven and the cracks under the door were rather large. While I was in the bathroom, the kids would not only push notes under the door, but they would push actual toys, like Matchbox cars and Tinker Toys! Now I can laugh about it, but looking back at those days, I was overwhelmed. Mothering is an intense, around-the-clock job, and solitude is not something that just happens by chance. We have to create it.

PRACTICE SOLITUDE IN SEASON

I've lived in the Midwest my entire life. In the winter here, we have forced dormancy. We must stay inside while outside the plants and animals rest. Come springtime, these plants and animals display the majesty of their Creator. In the same way, we women need forced dormant moments where we come inside to be alone with God. We need quiet and unproductive moments in order to be women living well who are drinking deep from the living well—Jesus.

We need time alone to read God's Word.

We need time alone to pray.

It may feel unproductive to slow down and get alone with God, but come springtime, we will display the majesty of the Creator when we have rested with Jesus!

It is in times of solitude that God refuels us and we can hear His voice. In our restful times we can find order in the midst of chaos and connect with our Creator.

Are you getting enough solitude? If you are feeling inpatient, irritable, bitter, forgetful, disorganized, or disconnected from God—it's time to take care of your soul. Grab your Bible and get alone with God!

JESUS' EXAMPLE OF SOLITUDE

- Jesus inaugurated His ministry by spending forty days alone in the desert (Matt. 4:1–11).
- Before Jesus chose the twelve disciples, He spent the entire night alone (Luke 6:12).
- When the disciples had finished a long day with the crowds, Jesus instructed them, "Come away by yourselves to a desolate place and rest a while" (Mark 6:31).
- Following the healing of the leper, Jesus withdrew alone to the wilderness to pray (Luke 5:16).

If Jesus needed solitude, then certainly we do too. When we forgo our own needs, including our own need for solitude, we not only shortchange ourselves but our families as well.

Rarely does anyone tell us to get alone and put our feet up, go read a good book, or take a warm bubble bath. We mistakenly believe that we can keep charging ahead like the Energizer bunny, without consequence. It seems our to-do lists are too long and the needs of our family are too great for us to ever take a break.

Drink from the Living Well

The Word of God is full of living water. We need to drink deeply from this living well so we can be women living well. Jesus said to the woman at the well in John 4:13–14, "Everyone who drinks of this water [physical water from the well] will be thirsty again, but whoever drinks of the water that I will give him will never be thirsty again. The water that I will give him will become in him a spring of water welling up to eternal life."

The Bible is revolutionary, life-changing, extraordinary, eye-opening, jaw-dropping, and downright amazing. It is filled with romance, tragedy, heroes, good, and evil. There is suspense, drama, wisdom, and comfort. As you read, you will weep and you will jump for joy. Yet we women are too often drawn away by novels, self-help books, cookbooks, magazines, and social media. These are a poor substitute for the Bible and a relationship with God.

Other reading materials steal our time away from the *one* book that is most extraordinary on the planet—the Bible. Those books and magazines are inviting and enjoyable—and don't get me wrong: you may just see me reading one on the beach—but they lack the power of God's voice.

It's only in the Bible that we find direct words from God. There is no other place in this world where we can get a direct message from God, so why do we neglect reading Scripture? Don't we want to hear God's voice?

I charge my cell phone daily because without power it goes dead. Similarly, we need to plug into God's power daily. We need to be recharged by His words and His strength daily. Reading God's Word every day will change the entire course of our lives.

Just as we cannot charge our cell phone only once a week, being recharged in God's Word is not a once-a-week assignment. The Bible is not something we read in church on Sunday and then close and tuck away on a shelf until the following Sunday. God wants us to drink deeply of His living water every day. He wants us to find refreshment, comfort, and satisfaction through His Word. David used the analogy of a deer: "As a deer pants for flowing streams, so pants my soul for you, O God" (Ps. 42:1).

Are we thirsting for Jesus, or have we made ourselves so busy that we don't even know our soul's greatest need—solitude with God?

Do you want to be a better wife? Study your Bible.

Do you want to be a better mother? Study your Bible.

Do you want to be a better homemaker? Study your Bible.

Do you want to be a better friend or coworker? Study your Bible.

So let's begin our hike toward being women living well by drinking from the living well of God.

Follow me through this heavenly hike together as we learn and discern how to walk with the King!

2

NO TIME FOR A
QUIET TIME

*The discipline to rise early is not as difficult as the
discipline of going to bed. This did not used to be so. Before
electricity and radio and television and the Internet,
going to bed soon after dark was not so difficult. There
was not much to do. Today the strongest allurements to
stay up and be entertained are against us. Therefore,
the battle against weariness, which makes us drowsy
as soon as we open our Bible in the morning, has to
be fought in the evening, not just in the morning.*

—JOHN PIPER, *WHEN I DON'T DESIRE GOD*

When I was in the fourth grade, my mother taught me how to have a quiet time alone with God each day. I remember plopping down on my pink frilly bed in my pink frilly room and opening my Bible and my journal. The journal was marked with tabs for prayer requests, verses to memorize, and pages to write my daily reading and thoughts. I felt so grown-up studying my Bible just like my big sisters. Finally, I could do my quiet times grown-up style—no more children's Bibles with pictures! Recently, I found a journal from 1986. Inside the journal my mother had jotted notes to me—she encouraged me, corrected me, and helped point me toward holiness. Love is spilled all over those pages—the love of a mother for her daughter and the love of two sisters in Christ, striving to follow God.

The first Bible I remember treasuring as my own was my Rainbow Bible that I received as a teenager. It was a unique study Bible that had a color-coding system printed on every page. For example, verses about God, Jesus, and the Holy Spirit were highlighted purple. Verses about love, kindness, mercy, sympathy, and comfort were highlighted green. Verses about sin, evil, temptation, or unbelief were highlighted gray. There were twelve different colors used to code every verse in the Bible, and not only did this help me as I studied my Bible, but it made me proud to carry it to school every day! My Bible was pretty when you opened it, and often it would pique my friends' curiosity and allow me the chance to share God's Word with them.

During those teen years, I moved into my older sister's bedroom. She had left the house, and I was thrilled to have her bigger room. I had left the pink frills behind and moved into a more mature yellow bedroom, and this bed was my landing place to get alone with God. I also discovered a tiny corporate park two minutes from my home. The park seemed to have people in it only during the lunch hour, so it was usually empty. The sound of the fountain running in the little pond brought me tranquillity. Here, I could meet alone with God to pray. Oftentimes on my drive home from school, I would turn into the park, walk across a little bridge, and sit down on a rock by a stream and talk and listen to God. I would return to this "prayer rock" many times throughout my young adult life and eventually with my boyfriend to pray and read Christian books together. During this season of life, I would go alone to pray about my boyfriend, who later became my husband.

SEARCHING FOR SOLITUDE IN
LIFE'S CHANGING SEASONS

Then it was time to move to Chicago for college. My suitcases were overflowing with hopes and dreams of growing closer to God in the big city. I moved into the dormitory with hundreds of other young women buzzing around like bees, and the reality of the challenge to find a place to get alone with God began. Finding a park with a prayer rock in the middle of downtown Chicago was not an option! But one day I discovered a quiet place in my dorm: the stairwell. On hard days, when I needed to get away and pray, cry, or read God's Word, I would climb ten flights to the top of the stairwell. There I'd sit beside the door that opened to the roof and would find refreshing solitude and communion with God.

After graduating from college, I got married and began my first full-time job. Everything in my life had changed, except my longing to get alone with God. I continued to find quiet pockets of time with Jesus by sitting in my car during lunch break or scattering out my Bible study books all over our kitchen table.

Then it happened—I hit the driest and hardest season of my life in my walk with God. I think this is when the hike began. I gave birth to two little sweet peas, and my bundles of joy exhausted me, and for the first time in my life, my consistent daily walk with God became a struggle. Heading to the nearest park, stairwell, or even my car was not an option. My babies needed my full attention when they were awake, and when they were sleeping I seemed to always have something on my plate that kept me "too busy."

My hunger and thirst for God did not die . . . I just couldn't seem to find the time to sit and linger long with my precious Savior or keep my eyes open when I did find those quiet moments. I would try to line up the kids' naps in the afternoon to sneak in a quiet time, and inevitably one would wake too soon or not want to go to sleep, and I would end up frustrated. Another factor during the baby season was my husband's work schedule. He traveled extensively, and there seemed to be no room to breathe, much less to get alone with God. It was during one of my hard days that I realized I *had* to get a babysitter for three hours a week when my husband traveled so I could find a quiet place.

"But he [Jesus] would withdraw to desolate places and pray" (Luke 5:16).

Once my babysitter arrived, I headed to the nearest library, coffee shop, or restaurant and savored my sweet moments of solitude.

I learned that I could not throw in the towel when the hike with God got tough. It was this duty of listening to God's voice in His Word and prayer that maintained my daily life. Time with God was as crucial to me as breathing. But the ideal of rising early, being well rested, wide-awake, and all alone with a hot drink in my hand, while basking in the presence of God, was met with a rude awakening.

Instead, my new reality went something like this: The alarm would go off, and I'd hit the snooze button. Five short minutes later the alarm would go off again, and I'd drag my sorry self out of bed. I'd somehow find my way to the kitchen and pull out my Bible and journal. I'd go to the cupboard to get out a mug, and lo and behold: a fuzzy-haired sweet pea would be staring at me. I'd look into those sleepy eyes and say, "Sweetheart, go back to bed; it's very early, and Mommy needs her quiet time." And from behind her would be the giggle of my other child. Argh! How could they both be up and with so much energy? "Please, oh please, give Mommy just five minutes alone with Jesus!"

MEDITATE ON GOD'S WORD

Some days a scheduled quiet time just can't happen. And it would be wrong for us to put pressure on ourselves to always create this perfect scenario—as we would selfishly have to push our children's needs aside.

So what's the solution?

Learn how to meditate on God's Word. Joshua 1:8 says, "This Book of the Law shall not depart from your mouth, but *you shall meditate on it day and night*, so that you may be careful to do according to all that is written in it."

Meditating is essentially soaking in God's Word. Like a sponge, sit and linger over God's Word. Take in the living water and be refreshed. Meditating goes hand in hand with memorization. If you are memorizing, then most likely you are also meditating. But it is possible to meditate and not memorize.

A Busy Mom's Guide to Meditating on a Passage of Scripture

1. *Choose a passage of Scripture for the week.* My favorite passages to meditate on come from Psalms, Proverbs, Ecclesiastes, and the Gospels. I also love the reading plans offered at GoodMorningGirls.org—they are my go-to Bible reading guides.[1]

2. *Write the passage on a note card and slip it in your pocket.* Pull it out periodically and read over it. Keep it in your purse all week long, and pull it out at convenient times and read through it.

3. *Open your Bible to that passage, and place it on the kitchen counter.* All day long, when you walk through the kitchen, pause, read the passage, and then move on.

4. *Read the passage out loud.* Read it to yourself, and read it to the children during breakfast and lunchtime.

5. *Read the passage first thing in the morning.* Read the passage as soon as you get out of bed so it's the first thing on your mind that morning.

6. *Read the passage before you go to bed at night.* Bookend your days with the reading of this passage of Scripture.

> 7. *Write the verses at the top of your to-do list.* This way, every time you look over your to-do list, you can review the Scripture passage.

Squeeze *every* drop of nourishment out of the passage all day long through these short readings of Scripture. Meditate on God's Word day and night, and you will soon find your life transformed by the renewing of your mind!

If You Fail to Plan, You're Planning to Fail

If you don't have a plan for dinner, most likely you'll be scrambling for something edible at the last minute. If you don't make plans the night before for what you will wear to church, you probably will end up at church late or in wrinkled clothes. If you don't have a plan to keep up with your friends' birthdays, you'll be buying a lot of belated cards. Bible study is the same way. Planning makes all the difference.

So what things could we plan that would make the discipline of a quiet time easier?

Plan When

Choose when you will have a quiet time each day. We are creatures of habit, so select a time that works best in your season of life, and work toward being disciplined at that time. One of my strongest memories from childhood is of my mother studying her Bible late at night at the kitchen table. When my children were babies, I was more alert in the afternoons, so that's when I tried to have my quiet times. There are many great Christian heroes of the faith down through the ages who had early-morning quiet times, including David (Ps. 5:3) and Daniel (Dan. 6:10). In Mark 1:35, we see Jesus spending time with His Father in the morning: "And rising very early in the morning, while it was still dark, he departed and went out to a deso-late place, and there he prayed."

One of my favorite authors, Elizabeth George, encourages women to "beat your family up."[2] Of course she doesn't mean to use physical force. She means to rise earlier than they do so you can have a few moments of solitude. There is a small window of time in the morning that slams shut the moment your children wake. So even if you can only rise five minutes early, grab that five minutes and delight in your devotions with your heavenly Father. He loves you so!

Plan Where

Plan your solitary place. As a newlywed, I felt a need to create a "prayer closet," so in our apartment I turned a walk-in closet into a prayer closet. Matthew 6:6 says, "When you pray, go into your room and shut the door and pray to your Father who is in secret. And your Father who sees in secret will reward you."

In the closet, I put a chair and footstool bought at a bargain outlet store; a cheap nightstand filled with my journal, Bible, and hymnal; and a little water fountain and CD player in the corner, along with some photos of loved ones. This was the most inviting solitary place I've ever had.

One of the only solitary rooms in our home now is the bath-room. In our first home, I turned my vanity in the master bathroom into my sanctuary! Some might imagine a sanctuary to have stained-glass windows and a pipe organ—but the word *sanctuary* simply means "holy place." I wanted a holy place in my home where I could step away from the kids, pray, and meet with God. We took down the mirror, and I put up a dry-erase board. Then, rather than using the drawers for makeup and accessories, I filled them with devotional books, highlighters, my Bible, and planner, and set my computer on the countertop.

I have worked hard to create an escape from the distractions of life to be alone with God. I encourage you to create a place that is inviting and that is ready and waiting for you. Maybe you have a chair in the family room that you could use and place a basket beside it with all your quiet-time goodies. Or maybe, like my mom, you prefer the kitchen table!

Plan How

Plan how you will have your quiet time. There are many ways to study God's Word. Here are a few suggestions:

- Follow the ideas for meditation we've already discussed. Write out your verses of the week on a note card or keep your Bible open in the kitchen to this passage.
- Follow a yearly Bible reading plan. Biblestudytools.com has a helpful tool where you can custom build your reading plan.
- There are thirty-one chapters in Proverbs. Read a proverb a day for each day of the month.
- Read with a pen in your hand. If there is something you are dealing with in your life, as you read, mark the passages that speak to you.
- Use colored pencils and a symbol system. Highlighters can bleed through the pages, so colored pencils work well. This is how my mother studies her Bible. She marks key words in passages, such as the word *Lord*, which is always marked with a yellow triangle. The word *blood* is marked with a red teardrop. The word *holy* is marked with a symbol of orange fire.
- Use a five-subject notebook to journal what you are learning. I like to journal my thoughts and applications, key verses, quotes from books I am reading, prayers, and confessions.
- Use the SOAP method to study a book of the Bible. This is the method we use at GoodMorningGirls.org. Good Morning Girls is an online, in-depth Bible study tailored for the busy woman who wants to be in God's

Word but not walk the road alone. We provide free Bible reading plans, e-books, videos, extra resources, and even small accountability groups. Every day we write a few verses in our journals. Then we look over the verses and write down a few things we learn from the passage—for example, a command, a promise, or an observed attribute about God. Then we ask ourselves, how does this apply to my daily life now? We write out a few applications. We close our time in prayer by praying the passage or the applications over our own lives and the lives of those we love. Here's a simpler explanation:

- S—Write out the Scripture passage for the day.
- O—Write down one or two observations from the passage.
- A—Write down one to two applications from the passage.
- P—Pray over what you learned from today's passage.

- Do a word study. Determine what you would like to know more about from God's Word. It may be something you struggle with, like anger, worry, fear, joy, or forgiving others. It may be a theological area you'd like to study, like grace, faith, sanctification, or the return of Jesus. Maybe you'd like to look into family matters, like what God says about children, marriage, or homemaking. Whatever it is, write that down in your journal.

   Go online to a website such as BibleGateway.com to research this topic. You can search by keyword, and all the verses in the Bible that contain the word you are searching will pop up. For example, there are 268 verses with the word *anger*. Now skim through those verses and write down the verses that pertain to your situation or what you are looking to know more about.

Take the verses you wrote down and look up each one in its context to see what God has to say about the word you are studying. Write down what you observe and how you can apply it. Memorize the verse that speaks the most strongly to your heart.

How to Do an Advanced Word Study

- Look up the definition of the word in the Greek or Hebrew in a concordance or Bible dictionary.
- Read the verses in a few different versions of the Bible.
- Research further information in a commentary, such as *Matthew Henry's Commentary on the Whole Bible*.

All these tools are available at Biblestudytools.com. This website is the most comprehensive that I have found, and I've spent hours on there, learning God's Word—so check it out and enjoy!

Memorize Scripture

Pick a passage that's meaningful to you. Meditate on it—study it—ingest it! Write it on sticky notes or index cards. Then put them in the bathroom, kitchen, by your computer, and in your car. Be intentional.

Get the entire family memorizing, and chart your progress on the refrigerator. Draw a picture of the verse you are memorizing—this is my favorite technique for teaching young kids memory verses! Give out stars for progress.

Count how many words there are in the verse—write it out that number of times, and you'll know it! Be sure to memorize where it is found. Practice, practice, practice—and before you know it the verses will overflow out of your mouth, and you will be armed with the Word of God!

Once you have memorized the verse, send it as a lunch note or in an e-mail to a friend. The more times you write it, the more it will sink in.

Purchase a Bible Study Book

If you want to read the Bible with someone guiding you through your study, there are many resources available both online and at all Christian bookstores.

TOO BUSY TO SIT STILL

The reality is we live in a busy culture where it is hard to simply sit still at the feet of Jesus.

My son has always been a very active little guy and not much of a cuddler. From the day he began walking, he no longer wanted to sit in my lap. I would try to hold him and cuddle him, and he would straighten his arms and slip to the floor. He wanted to be free! But that made me sad, because I longed for lingering moments, like when he was a baby.

Sometimes I act this way with God. He desires to spend time alone with me. He wants me to be still and enjoy Him. But no, I want to be free. Free to run around distracted and doing my own thing.

God doesn't want to hold us down all day long, but He does want just a little while to linger with us. He wants to tell us how much He loves us and guide us by His Word. He wants us to talk to Him about our day, our struggles, and our needs. He wants to teach us. He wants to reveal to us areas we need to mature in and fill us up with love, joy, and hope. He wants to be thanked and worshipped. He wants us to be still and know that He is God (Ps. 46:10).

I think back to those fourth-grade days, when lingering with God on my pink frilly bed came so easily, and now I look at the silent battle waging in my soul. I have to fight for time alone with God in the midst of my busy calendar. I have to plan what I'm going to read for the month. I have to get up in the dark hours of the early morning to find the only solitary moment in my day. My Bible is always waiting for me in the center of the kitchen table—calling out to me, *Come drink this cup of living water, for only this will satisfy your thirst.*

This is why we meet with God. He loves us so much He hung on a cross for us so we could be forgiven of all our heinous sins. Certainly we can set aside a few minutes a day to walk with the King.

3

HOW THIRSTY AM I?

Behind the passionate life of every passionate saint is a passion for God and His Word.

—Elizabeth George, *Life Management for Busy Women*

Every morning I wake up before the family, brew a cup of coffee, and sit at the kitchen table with my Bible. My kitchen faces east, so most mornings there's a glorious sunrise out my window. I have the perfect setting for meeting with Jesus . . . except there's one problem. Me! I can't focus. My mind seems to wander everywhere but to God's Word and prayer.

At times, my prayer life feels like a wrestling match. Have you experienced this? You sit down to pray, and within one minute your brain is distracted? I start thinking about my to-do list, or I get interrupted by the kids, or worse, I drift off to sleep! Yes, a thousand invisible enemies seem to fill the air the minute I sit down to pray.

I have found one solution to this problem in my life: prayer journaling.

For twenty years I have kept a prayer journal. I started when I was sixteen, daily writing down my prayer requests and praises.

Then when I was in college, my journal morphed and I began to include confessions along with my prayer requests and praises. At times I wrote only my prayer list for the day, and other times I wrote a long letter to God, pouring my heart out to Him in the form of a written prayer.

My journals have never been fancy or costly. I usually use a five-subject notebook for the year and a ballpoint pen. At the top of each page, I write the date, and then I write an overflow of my heart to God. It's in these silent moments that I share with God my joys, hurts, anger, sadness, delights, passions, and prayers for friends, for family, and for lost loved ones. Often I include deep thoughts I heard or read that day, a verse that touched my heart, or a memory that I don't want to forget.

Although I am a modern-day homemaker and not an ancient-shepherd-boy-turned-king, my journals read like David's psalms. Sometimes I cry to God in the midst of a terrible time, and other times I write a hymn of praise that overflows from my heart.

Edith Schaeffer wrote of journaling, "God has communicated with us in writing. His Word, the Bible. . . . So writing our pleas, our praise, our prayers—this is not a one-sided communication. God will hear, and He will answer. . . . It's a relaxed and protected comforting communication with one's Father, Shepherd, Friend, Counselor and mighty God. He is Personal—and therefore we can speak and write to Him in a personal and intimate communication."[1]

PACING MY HOME; WHISPERING MY PRAYERS

If you were to have a camera rigged up in my home, this is what you might see on an ordinary day in my life as I venture on a prayer walk through my home:

My prayer walk begins as I pull up the crumpled blankets on my bed from the night's rest: "Lord, bless the man who slept here last night—give him strength for today's trials, integrity for today's temptations, and wisdom for today's decisions."

I go around to the other side of the bed and pull the blankets up: "Lord, help me be a blessing to my husband today, help me be patient with the children, and help me be wise for today's challenges."

I walk into the bathroom, where bathtub toys are strewn across the floor. I pick up the Matchbox car: "Lord, bless my little boy, who dreams big and plays hard. Help him use his strength for You."

I lay my daughter's bath baby back into the bucket: "Lord, bless my little girl. She has so many words to say; help her be wise in her word choices."

I walk to the kitchen and wipe crumbs from the morning breakfast table: "Lord, use this table to comfort weary souls along life's journey."

I wipe the first chair: "Lord, help my leader husband to be healthy so he can complete the ever-mounting tasks on his plate."

I wipe the second and third chairs: "Lord, give the children laughter in their adventures together. Knit their souls together in peace and love."

And then the fourth chair: "Lord, help . . . I just need help." Tears bubble under the surface. No more words need to be said. The Spirit understands what words cannot express.

Then into the living room, I straighten pillows and say prayers for visitors, friends, and family who once sat there. I wipe dust from the piano as praise bellows in my heart for the joy that has come through the blessing of that black wooden box with ivory keys. Memories of children singing and dancing flood my heart with joy. But the joy is broken as I lift the newspaper from the entryway. The world's troubles are thrust upon me—I lift prayers for my city, state, country, and president.

My heart is heavy as I lift the heavy laundry basket and carry it out of the room and up the stairs. The basket seems to get lighter as I thank the Lord for giving us these clothes in abundance. I open the drawer and slip the clothes into their comfy home, ready to be used.

I walk past the television and pause: "Lord, have we dishonored

You by the things we have watched on TV? Help us not to waste our time on useless viewing, which turns into useless living."

I walk to my computer. There it sits . . . the world at my fingertips . . . it woos me to come and sit for a while.

My Bible is right beside the keyboard. There it sits, God's only written Word there at my fingertips. It, too, woos me to come and sit for a while.

Why am I so torn? Why does the computer's wooing seem stronger than the Bible's? I pause for repentance: "Father, forgive me for weak moments, where time spent on my computer has caused me to neglect Your Word."

I open my Bible and drink the living water that is spilled on every page. Sweet refreshment. I rise as little voices call out, "Mommy!" Temptations to carry my heavy burden rise with me. I move forward, leaving my burden to lie at the feet of Jesus. My heart is light; I walk in peace. I walk with the King, and the King walks with me.

I encourage you to take the time to pray over your loved ones, over the places they sleep, their toys, the television that will capture them for as long as you allow, and the computer that can bring life or death into your home. Let God use a daily prayer walk to transform your family. If you don't pray for them, who will?

My Faith Crisis

I have never been one to doubt God or His Word. I've always prayed in confidence, knowing that God loves me and hears my prayers. But five years ago, my husband and I were traveling, and we had a long layover in the Dallas/Fort Worth airport. The place was packed! All the chairs were taken, so we found a spot on the floor, and I leaned against the wall and began people watching.

For an hour, I watched hundreds of people hustling and bustling every which way to get to their gates. Mamas were feeding their children, babies were crying, and businessmen were reading their newspapers. And in that moment I had a faith crisis.

I thought, *Lord, look at all these people. Do You really hear my prayers? How do You hear the prayers of all the people who pray to You? Are You really thinking of me? Am I really on Your heart and mind? When I think of all the billions of people in this world, I can't understand how You could see me.*

I was troubled in my Spirit for not trusting, yet my mind could not comprehend how God hears everyone's prayers at the same time—suddenly I wasn't so sure He was listening.

The next morning I awoke in Los Cabos, Mexico, and I went out on my balcony to have my quiet time. The view of the ocean, birds, flowers, and sunrise was magnificent. I wiped the pile of sand from my chair with my hand, sat down, and opened my Bible to Psalm 139 and began reading. When I came to verses 17 and 18, I paused:

How precious to me are your thoughts, O God!
How vast is the sum of them!
If I would count them, they are more than the sand.
I awake, and I am still with you.

Back that train up; I had to read those verses again. David said that if he were to count the number of times God thinks of him, the sum would be greater than the number of grains of sand! David had full confidence that he was on God's mind. I want to be like David, whom God referred to as "a man after my heart" (Acts 13:22).

I reflected and I looked at the grains of sand still stuck on my hand from wiping the chair. Then I glanced at the pile of sand that had fallen to the floor. Then I looked in the cracks and crevices of the balcony—there were hundreds of grains of sand collected there. I looked up over the balcony to where the flowers were blooming— loads of sand dotted the flower beds. I looked out to the ocean, where the sandy beach spread for miles . . . hundreds of thousands of millions and trillions of grains of sand. And in that moment, tears filled my eyes and my heart filled with praise. My God *does* hear my prayers!

And so I wonder, are you waiting on God for an answer to your prayer? Do you wonder if God really hears your prayers? God's Word says yes, He hears you! He loves you, and you are on His mind and on His heart.

WAIT TRAINING

During the season of waiting on God to answer our prayers, our faith sometimes begins to waver. The silence from God can be deafening, and our patience can quickly fade. But we see in God's Word that His children have been called to wait on Him time and time again.

In the Bible we are told that Abraham waited until he was one hundred years old for his promised son (Gen. 21:5). Joshua marched around the walls of Jericho and waited for seven days before God brought the walls down (Josh. 6:20). Daniel waited to be delivered in the lions' den (Dan. 6). Israel waited for their Messiah to come. Mary waited nine months for Jesus to be born, and Jesus waited three days in the tomb to rise again.

If you are waiting on God in prayer, remember Isaiah 40:28–31:

> Have you not known? Have you not heard?
> The LORD is the everlasting God,
> the Creator of the ends of the earth.
> He does not faint or grow weary;
> his understanding is unsearchable.
> He gives power to the faint,
> and to him who has no might he increases strength.
> Even youths shall faint and be weary,
> and young men shall fall exhausted;
> but they who wait for the LORD shall renew their strength;
> they shall mount up with wings like eagles;
> they shall run and not be weary;
> they shall walk and not faint.

ECHOES OF SILENCE

But what if you are diligent to pray, and pray, and then pray some more—and still you receive no answer, just silence? I have received many gut-wrenchingly painful e-mails from women who are suffering in a season of unanswered prayers. Psalm 121:1–3 is a passage of Scripture I turn to when I'm struggling with unanswered prayer:

> I lift up my eyes to the hills.
> From where does my help come?
> My help comes from the LORD,
> who made heaven and earth.
> He will not let your foot be moved;
> he who keeps you will not slumber.

God does not sleep. He is always in control. He will not let our feet slip. We must persevere in prayer.

I tell my children often, "God is always watching, He is always listening, and He cares for you." I pray that one day when I am not there to comfort their hurts, this truth will be so ingrained in their minds that they will sense the ultimate Comforter there with them.

This Comforter is the Holy Spirit. Jesus says in John 14:16–17, "And I will ask the Father, and he will give you another Helper, to be with you forever, even the Spirit of truth, whom the world cannot receive, because it neither sees him nor knows him. You know him, for he dwells with you and will be in you."

In the Greek the word translated "another" in this verse means "another who is exactly the same,"[2] and the word rendered "helper" is *parakletos*, meaning "comforter, one called alongside to help."[3]

If you are hurting, you may feel all alone in your trials and difficulties. But you are not. Jesus has sent "another" counselor with the same mind, emotions, intellect, and wisdom into our hearts to guide, comfort, direct, and help us manage our way through life.

Have you yielded to this Counselor, the Holy Spirit? You must

first be in God's Word, in prayer, and in stillness to sense His clear
leading, comfort, and guidance. If you are hurting today, practice
the presence of God in your life. Psalm 139:7–10 says:

> Where shall I go from your Spirit?
> Or where shall I flee from your presence?
> If I ascend to heaven, you are there!
> If I make my bed in Sheol, you are there!
> If I take the wings of the morning
> and dwell in the uttermost parts of the sea,
> even there your hand shall lead me,
> and your right hand shall hold me.

Know that God is always with you. Surrender your will to Him.
Be still, listen, and move forward in peace.

WHEN OUR THIRST FOR GOD CANNOT BE QUENCHED

When our soul aches, our to-do list is a mile long, and we can't hear
God over the noise of our technology, then what?

It's time to fast.

Fasting is a spiritual discipline that feeds our souls while we
starve our bodies. Every time our minds signal *I want food*, it's a signal for us instead to pray.

As Americans, to give up food from sundown to sundown is not
an easy task. When it comes to fasting, Diet Coke is hands-down the
hardest thing to deny myself for twenty-four hours! But how hungry
for God are we?

John Piper wrote in *A Hunger for God*:

> When midmorning comes and you want food so badly that the
> thought of lunch becomes as sweet as summer vacation, then
> suddenly you realize, "Oh, I forgot, I made a commitment. I can't

have that pleasure. I'm fasting for lunch too." Then what are you going to do with all the unhappiness inside? Formerly, you blocked it out with the hope of a tasty lunch. The hope of food gave you the good feelings to balance out the bad feelings. But now the balance is off. You must find another way to deal with it.[4]

Fasting is a servant. In its quiet moments, it brings out your soul's struggles. The hope of a bag of chips or a gallon of ice cream to drown your sorrows is stripped away, and you find yourself raw before God's throne.

On days of fasting for me, I do not watch any television and have minimal computer time or texting. Sometimes I fast with friends, so we will text and e-mail each other encouragement throughout the day. But otherwise, it's a quiet day. There is nothing and no one to conceal my dark feelings. It is there, before God's throne, that I find time and time again that indeed God is enough.

In the Bible, we see many great men and women of God fasting in prayer. There's Moses, Hannah, David, Jehoshaphat, Ezra, Nehemiah, Esther, Daniel, Joel, Zechariah, Paul, and our ultimate example—Jesus.

Have you tried fasting yet? It's a spiritual discipline that many neglect. Our fast-paced society doesn't leave a lot of space for slowing down to pray. It takes discipline and intentional planning to do it well.

Tips for a Twenty-Four-Hour Fast

- *Set aside twenty-four hours when you'll be home most of the day.* Note: do not fast if you are pregnant or have a medical condition that requires a special diet.
- *Go from sundown to sundown.* I like to eat an early supper on day one, but the next evening it is such a joy to break the fast with family!

- *Fasting is not to impress God or others.* Fasting was created by God as a tool to bring us into a closer relationship with Him.
- *Without prayer, fasting is simply a diet.* You must commit to praying and meditating during the times you would normally eat a meal.

Are you hungering and thirsting for God? Sometimes the only way to quench this spiritual thirst is to fast.

LIVING THE SATISFIED LIFE

My babies loved their pacifiers. The word *pacify* means "to stop agitation, to soothe, appease, or subdue."[5] What would happen if I gave my babies a pacifier and never gave them a bottle? They could not survive. They'd be pacified, but their stomachs would not be satisfied. The bottle of milk is what truly satisfies them. *Satisfied* is "being completely happy and at peace, all requirements are met."[6]

What do you use to pacify yourself? For some it's pleasure or fun—you seek an adrenaline rush. Others are consumed with their current romantic relationships or seeking another one. Some seek beauty, to be in style, to have power, or to be in control of everything in their lives. Still others seek money and possessions; you dream of a nicer car or a bigger house and believe that if you had those things, then you'd be happy.

In Ecclesiastes, King Solomon took a hard look into the meaning of life. He observed man's human efforts apart from God to achieve happiness, wisdom, money, and pleasure. He declared these efforts to be meaningless and "a striving after wind" (1:14). The end result of seeking money, pleasure, beauty, or any of the others is the same: painful unfulfillment. The most obvious symptom of a soul in need of God's satisfaction is a sense of inner emptiness—the constant inability to be satisfied.

In seeing Jesus, we see our source of fulfillment. He offers love, joy, peace, mercy, grace, forgiveness, acceptance, hope, and so much more than the world can ever offer us.

Let me ask you a question. Is your soul, your spirit, the real you, pacified by worldly things, or entirely satisfied in Jesus? Can you say you are full, content, and all requirements are met by Jesus alone?

Do you know Jesus? We all know the Christmas story: a young virgin gave birth to a baby in a stable in Bethlehem. He lived a perfect life, but the temple rulers hated Him because multitudes followed Him everywhere He went. He was healing blind men, raising people from the dead, feeding five thousand people with only five loaves of bread and two fish. The more people followed Him, the more the Jewish leaders hated Him, until the day they arrested Him, put Him on trial for saying He was God, and nailed Him to the cross.

Jesus laid down His life. If He could heal a blind man and stop a raging storm at sea, He certainly could have gotten away from those who crucified Him, but the Bible says He laid down His life as the payment for our sins (Rom. 5:8–11). Before Jesus died on the cross, the men of the family had to sacrifice a lamb at the temple, and the lamb's blood would cover the sins of their family. But Jesus was the final sacrifice, and His blood has covered our sins.

After they laid Him in a tomb, three days later He rose again, proving that He indeed is God.

Do you believe that? The Bible says if you repent and believe (Mark 1:15), then your soul is saved. And when this body dies, your soul will go to heaven (John 3:16).

But have you felt it? Have you felt a fight for your soul? The battle is huge in this high-tech society! As we have seen, there are voices everywhere, with televisions, iPods, computers, radios, cell phones, and more competing for our attention. These voices distract us from hearing the voice of God and dealing with our spiritual issues.

I'm sure you have felt the exhaustion, fatigue, and the drain on your emotional and spiritual life as you balance being a wife, mother, and everything else you have to do.

When we are stressed, we can look to a lot of things to feed our souls, such as a fun girls' night out or a long movie or time surfing on the Web or a huge batch of chocolate chip cookies! But anything less than God Himself will leave our souls unsatisfied.

Psalm 63 says:

> O God, you are my God; earnestly I seek you;
> my soul thirsts for you;
> my flesh faints for you,
> as in a dry and weary land where there is no water. . . .
> [But when I have you]
> my soul will be satisfied as with fat and rich food,
> and my mouth will praise you with joyful lips. (vv. 1, 5)

After eating your Thanksgiving turkey, stuffing, mashed potatoes, corn, cranberry sauce, roll, and then some pumpkin pie, your stomach is fully satisfied! And this is what David was saying his soul was like when he sought God: he was fully satisfied as with the richest of foods.

Are you that satisfied today with God?

John 6:35 says, "Jesus said to them, 'I am the bread of life; whoever comes to me shall not hunger, and whoever believes in me shall never thirst.'"

Is your soul thirsty? Walk with the King.

4

THE EFFECTS OF THE
MEDIA REVOLUTION

"I am the vine; you are the branches. Whoever
abides in me and I in him, he it is that bears much
fruit, for apart from me you can do nothing."

—JOHN 15:5

Times have changed. In Bible times, women met at the well to
chat with one another. Mary had to travel by foot or donkey
to visit Elizabeth. Some say she traveled eighty miles to visit her
cousin. It would have taken days to pass through this hill country.
But nowadays, this eighty-mile trip would take an hour and a half
in the car, or better yet, they could have simply Skyped each other!

Jesus lived in a different culture and context than we do. Never
before have women carried access to all the world's knowledge on a
tiny device in our purses! Screens are everywhere—at church, work,
gyms, on airplanes, in the car, and in our pockets. Twitter, Facebook,
Pinterest, blogging, and YouTube have become the new front porch
affecting all of our friendships. In just over sixty years, we've gone
from zero screen time to omnipresent screens—they are so ingrained
in the landscape of our culture that we don't even notice them!

Think of all the changes our generation has faced with the onslaught of the media revolution.

Maps are out; GPS systems are in.

CDs are out; iPods and iTunes are now the norm.

Phones with a cord attached to the wall are out; cell phones are how we chat.

Catalogs are out; e-mailed spam is in.

Handwritten notes are out; texting is in.

Classifieds are out; we buy and sell online now.

Travel agents are out; Internet travel deals are how we roam.

VCRs are out; Netflix and Redbox bring the movies home.

Our world is changing drastically and at breakneck speed. The world we grew up in looks nothing like the one in which our children are being raised.

As I step back and look at our media-saturated world, I see that we are a distracted generation. Beeps and chimes make us respond like Pavlov's dogs! No matter where we are—in the grocery store, church, the middle of dinner, or even driving—these chimes make us pick up our cell phones or run to our computers. We hope that something there will make us laugh, give us meaning, or make us feel loved.

Social Media and Our Spiritual Life

Media is amoral. In and of itself it is neither good nor evil. It is our use of it that determines its morality. Because there is no mention of this technology in the Bible, we must leave room for each believer to discern and follow his or her convictions on the use of media. But here are some of the negatives that have come with this media revolution.

Technology Can Distract Us from God

For nearly twenty years, I have risen early in the morning for prayer and Bible meditation. However, over the last few years I feel a tug toward my computer in the mornings. I have trouble being still and lingering over the refreshing water of the living Word! Rather than sipping it slowly, meditating, praying it over my family and friends, I gulp it down because I can hear the chimes—and I know overnight things have happened online. Once the online voices of the iPad and iPhone take over, the private meditation and conversation I have with the Great I AM come to an end.

Information Can Keep Us from Wisdom

As we seek wisdom online (and what a joy it is to connect with amazing men and women of faith!) may we never mistake information for wisdom. Unless we take the time to really contemplate what we are learning, write it down, pray over it, and live it out, much of the wisdom we read will be lost quickly out of our minds as we continue to read more information. We need time for pausing, processing, and serious consideration. This may mean reading less online or choosing just a few voices we listen to so we can take the time to live out what we have learned.

Multitasking Can Prevent Us from Focusing

Multitasking has become a virtue. But when it comes to our quiet time, this is *not* a time to be efficient! We do not want to speed through our daily devotions. We need to give God's Word quality and quantity time so it can be active in our lives.

"For the word of God is living and active, sharper than any two-edged sword, piercing to the division of soul and of spirit, of joints and of marrow, and discerning the thoughts and intentions of the heart" (Heb. 4:12).

Media Can Cost Us Precious Time

Media is designed to pull you in, to make you feel some sort of emotion: "Buy me; try me; watch me." It subtly persuades us. It intentionally molds us. It ultimately changes our thinking. Let me be honest: it has caused a time famine in my life. And this baffles me because everything around me is so efficient. My dishwasher washes my dishes while my laundry machines wash and dry my clothes. My car gets me places quickly, and my grocery store places chicken in plastic wrap, and I can purchase fruits and vegetables galore, rather than me having to raise the chickens or grow fruits and vegetables. So why do I have this famine of time? I can only attribute it to the time I've spent on media.

THE GREAT I AM

Have we forgotten the power of the "I"—not the iPad, iPhone, or iPod—but of the Great I AM? Jesus said:

- *"I am the bread of life*; whoever comes to me shall not hunger, and whoever believes in me shall never thirst" (John 6:35).
- *"I am the light of the world.* Whoever follows me will not walk in darkness, but will have the light of life" (John 8:12).
- *"I am the door.* If anyone enters by me, he will be saved and will go in and out and find pasture" (John 10:9).
- *"I am the good shepherd.* The good shepherd lays down his life for the sheep" (John 10:11).
- *"I am the resurrection and the life.* Whoever believes in me, though he die, yet shall he live" (John 11:25).
- *"I am the way, and the truth, and the life.* No one comes to the Father except through me" (John 14:6).
- *"I am the vine*; you are the branches. Whoever abides in me and I in him, he it is that bears much fruit, for apart from me you can do nothing" (John 15:5).

We have more voices speaking into our lives through the media revolution than ever before. Our generation and the generations to come will miss out on the voice of the Great I AM if we do not learn to be disciplined with our media intake. I believe it's affecting our ability to think clearly.

Elisabeth Elliot said, "Muddled thinking inevitably results in muddled living."[1] Because our thinking has become muddled by so much information, our living has become muddled. If we are not filtering all the information we take in through God's Word, we will lack the peace of God that guards our hearts and our minds, which we are promised in Philippians 4:7.

SOCIAL MEDIA AND OUR FRIENDSHIPS

Social media is the new front porch, and blogs are the new neighborhood. These new forms of communication can have positive and negative effects. I *love* social media because, well, I love to be social! I have thoroughly enjoyed getting to know friends in new ways through their status updates, links to things they find interesting, verses they post, and pictures from their daily lives. I have connected with strangers on Facebook and Twitter, and those strangers have become real-life, meaningful friends offline!

Actually, social media has nearly eliminated all my phone time in the home. If I have something to say to a friend, I hop onto Facebook and Twitter to "chat." I miss my friends who are not on Facebook (but respect their reasons) simply because I feel I have less access to them. I have to remember to be sensitive to their feelings of being left out. I have gotten closer to some of my acquaintances who are regulars on Facebook and Twitter because that's where I hang out when I need a break from cleaning or homeschooling!

But the convenience of social media comes with some dangers.

Hurt Feelings

I can't tell you the number of times I've read a comment on my blog or on a Facebook status update and have thought, *What does she mean? Is she mad at me? Is she joking around? Am I being too sensitive?* Online comments are dangerous—be careful, and think before you type! I am guilty of this too. Proverbs 26:18–19 says, "Like a madman who throws firebrands, arrows, and death is the man who deceives his neighbor and says, 'I am only joking!'" Beware of making sarcastic comments; you could lose a friendship over it.

Judging

I have friends who have closed their Facebook accounts because they were upset by status updates of friends whom they thought lived one way but they discovered lived a very different way. This is where sin and matters of liberty and conscience come into play. We must call sin, sin but give grace to our friends on matters of liberty. I will admit that bad language or inappropriate photos posted online mar my image of a friend. I, too, struggle with this at times.

I have learned that I am not on Facebook or Twitter to be everyone's Holy Spirit! That's a quick friendship killer that Satan thoroughly enjoys! Jesus, in John 10:10, says, "The thief comes only to steal and kill and destroy. I came that they may have life and have it abundantly." Satan would love to use social media to destroy our friendships, but Jesus came to give us an abundant life. Do not let sinful judgment of friends destroy your friendships. Remember, we are all human, and we are all in different places on our journeys with God.

Public Embarrassment

I will raise my hand first and say I've embarrassed myself publicly on many occasions because of my loose lips. In the moment, a status update or comment feels right, but the next day I wonder, *What in the world was I thinking?* Words carry power, and it's been a learning and maturing process on what to say publicly and what not to say. Proverbs 10:19 says, "When words are many, transgression is not lacking, but whoever restrains his lips is prudent."

Jealousy

The comparison trap is just that—a trap! Pictures of vacations, new homes, new cars, or fun nights out with friends are a breeding ground for jealousy. There are two sides to this coin. First, there's the person putting the information out there. Is it wrong to post a picture of your vacation or fun night out? *No* . . . but we can be sensitive to those who weren't invited or who can't afford a vacation this year. We don't have to post every picture or an update about every night out. Philippians 2:3–4 says, "In humility count others more significant than yourselves. Let each of you look not only to his own interests, but also to the interests of others." This is one reason I do not post large numbers of pictures from our family vacations on the blog. I want to be sensitive to the fact that not everyone will be happy to see those pictures.

On the flip side, jealousy is all throughout the Bible, and we see how deadly it is to friendships. Remember Cain and Abel, Sarah and Hagar, Joseph and his brothers, Haman and Mordecai, Saul and David, and the Pharisees and Jesus? These are just to name a few; if we looked into it further, we'd find many more relationships in the Bible that were ruined by jealousy. Jealousy comes when we take our eyes off Jesus.

When I feel discouraged by things happening in the social media world, I always come to a point of realizing that I have taken my eyes off Jesus. Hebrews 12:1–2 says, "Let us run with endurance the race that is set before us, *looking to Jesus*, the founder and perfecter of our faith." We must focus on Jesus and exchange drama for peace.

Inappropriate Relationships with Men

I am in no way suggesting that women cannot have friends who are men. But for me, I have decided to not have male friends on Facebook. I know that "the devil prowls around like a roaring lion, seeking someone to devour" (1 Peter 5:8), so I want to be alert and on guard. I am aware that I am a sinful human who is capable of being tempted and falling. I do not want to leave any known cracks in my life where he can sneak in.

INTERNET TIP

Follow this rule to filter what you share on the Internet:
Ask yourself, "If the pastor of my church put up on a large screen all the comments, status updates, and pictures I've posted for the entire congregation to see, is there anything that would embarrass me?"
This answer will reveal what you need to delete.

INFORMATION OVERLOAD

About a year into social media, I realized I was following too many people on Twitter, liking too many pages on Facebook, accepting too many friend requests, and subscribing to too many blogs. It was time to cut back. I went on Twitter and started unfollowing people. The people pleaser in me felt terrible.

Then I went to Facebook, and as I mentioned before, I deleted all my guy friends. Again, I felt awful doing it and hoped the guys wouldn't notice or take it personally. Then I prayed about which blogs I should subscribe to, and I unsubscribed to many of the blogs I was following. I went on Facebook and I "unliked" many of the pages I was following. This process was difficult for me, but in the end it was a huge relief.

I realized I was an information glutton. I was losing precious time trying to keep up with acquaintances, feeds, and blogs that were not beneficial to my real life. I was gathering more information than I could process or use, and all this information was crowding out the voice of God.

THE VOICE OF GOD

Information is a cheap substitute for the wisdom that comes from God. Since the garden of Eden, Satan has been tempting humankind to search for wisdom in all the wrong places. "When the woman saw that the tree was good for food, and that it was a delight to the eyes, and that the tree was to be desired to make one wise, she took of its fruit and ate, and she also gave some to her husband who was with her, and he ate" (Gen. 3:6).

Satan dangles his worldly knowledge before us in the form of online information, wooing us. God has not called His children to seek information; He calls us to seek Him. "And without faith it is impossible to please him, for whoever would draw near to God must believe that he exists and that *he rewards those who seek him*" (Heb. 11:6).

We no longer live in a day and age where women meet at the well to chat with other women. Now our family and friends are just a finger tap away. But before we open Facebook, we must go to the ultimate book, the Bible. Let's give God the first few minutes of our day.

It doesn't matter if we are reading a leather-bound Bible or using an iPad app to read God's Word. What matters is that we seek to walk with the King.

5

NEVER WALK ALONE

Going it alone is, without a doubt, one of the most common
and effective strategies that Satan uses to discourage moms.
A woman alone in her home with her ideals eventually wears
down and becomes a perfect target for Satan to discourage.

—SALLY CLARKSON, *DESPERATE*

I remember on weekends while in college in Chicago, when most of the girls went home or out on dates, I was homesick. I would sit in my dorm room alone, eating popcorn and listening to classical music for hours. I never went on a date in college. Not once. At the time I was dating Keith, my high school sweetheart, long-distance. I pored over God's Word on those long weekends and filled in the gaping hole of loneliness with God's presence.

Finally, I married Keith after four long years apart, and we moved to Columbus, Ohio, for him to finish college at Ohio State University. I was in a new town. With a new name. And a new job. And a new church. I recall walking into my first Bible study in the new church and no one greeting me. I sat alone and was very uncomfortable. I had made some non-Christian friends at work, but I longed for a safe refuge of Christian friends, where I could let down my guard, talk about spiritual things, and pray together. It took about eighteen months before I developed my first "real" Christian friendship. It was a long, lonely eighteen months.

LEADING WOMEN'S BIBLE STUDIES

After a year of attending women's Bible studies in my new church, I decided to step up to the plate and lead a women's Bible study. I still remember that first night of leading. My knees were knocking. My mouth was running a mile a minute (I talk faster when I'm nervous), and I'm sure the ladies in the study were wondering what on earth they'd gotten themselves into!

All of them were older than I was and had more life experience. I was a newlywed with no children, yet they graciously attended week in and week out, allowing me the honor of leading. We had a great time of fellowship, and real friendships were born. For the first time in my twenty-two years, I had friends decades older than I was but with no barrier of age. We were simply sisters journeying alongside one another on the road of life. We prayed together, cried together, went to dinner together, hugged one another, and encouraged one another. It was during this first Bible study that God opened my eyes to my passion to live in community with my sisters in Christ.

I still have a card from one woman twice my age who attended. In the note she expressed how she had her doubts about my ability to lead because of my age. But she stayed in the study and was pleasantly surprised how God blessed her every time we met!

I kept this card because her honesty touched me deeply. I was so young and green, but she gave me a chance. I was very insecure leading women's studies at such a young age, and I was troubled by the fact that I did not have life experience on my side as I taught God's Word. God would bring to mind 1 Timothy 4:12 time and time again to give me strength: "Let no one despise you for your youth, but set the believers an example in speech, in conduct, in love, in faith, in purity." So I pressed on with new ideas for community.

WOMAN TO WOMAN MENTORING MINISTRY

Holly and I met in our youth group at church when I was a freshman in high school and Holly was a junior. I was a public-schooled, chatty cheerleader with a hungry heart for more of Jesus in my life, and she was a homeschooled, sweet, quiet, strong spiritual role model. She took me under her wing and met with me weekly, giving me daily Bible reading assignments and holding me accountable for two years. Holly was my first mentor. Then off to Moody Bible Institute she went!

I longed to be like my mentor, so I visited her at Moody Bible Institute, and I loved it. Two years later I also enrolled there, following in her footsteps. There once again I was the immature freshman and she was the mature leader and resident adviser of our dorm floor. I often found myself sitting in her dorm room, pouring out my problems to her. Holly always had a Bible verse and prayer to share as she calmly reassured me of God's sovereignty. This girl was as cool as a cucumber through every trial and tribulation, standing firmly on God's Word. It was no surprise when she married and went overseas as a missionary to start her family.

Years later, I would sit in my Bible studies and wish I could provide mentors like Holly for the young women in my church. After research and a talk with my pastor, I sent letters to some spiritually mature women in my church. They read like this:

Dear (Potential Mentor),

We are beginning a new women's ministry called Woman to Woman Mentoring Ministry.[1] Our goal is for the women of our church to live out the Titus 2:3–5 mandate, "Older women likewise are to be reverent in behavior, not slanderers or slaves to much wine. They are to teach what is good, and so train the young women to love their husbands and children, to be self-controlled, pure, working at home, kind, and submissive to their own husbands, that the word of God may not be reviled."

We would like you to prayerfully consider being a mentor to

a spiritually younger woman. Your role would be one of encouraging, supporting, caring, and modeling the Christian life for a sister in Christ.

There is a lot of flexibility on how this can be done. We ask that you meet no less than twice a month. Sometimes you may meet together on a scheduled basis, such as once a week. Other times you may simply talk on the telephone or meet for lunch. One woman may need to learn how to love her husband and children while another may need you to focus on how to be busy at home and a better homemaker. Some women may need help in their walks with God or with purity as they encounter the different trials God has brought into their lives. Each mentorship will look distinctly different yet be fulfilling the same purpose of both discipleship and fellowship.

When the mentees sign up, they will have the option to choose what areas they would like to be mentored in, such as their walks with God, their marriages, raising their children, homemaking, finances, and their careers. We will match them according to what you feel are your strengths in these areas.

We ask that you spend the minimum of three months mentoring the mentee. At the end of three months, you will fill out an evaluation form and together decide if you'd like to continue on for the next three months.

These letters went out, and anxious prayers went up to the Lord. Soon the commitments came rolling in. Then for a few Sundays I stood at a table outside the sanctuary and prayed that ladies would sign up to be mentored. A beautiful mentorship ministry was born in our church that continues to this day.

Titus 2 Workshops

Once the mentorship ministry was off and rolling, I found there were fewer mentors than mentees, and this stirred my spirit to start a new ministry in our church, a ministry I titled "Titus 2 Workshops."

A couple of times a year, I would reserve a large room at our church and decorate it. I'd ask three "Titus 2" women to be on a panel and discuss subjects such as managing finances, cooking, parenting, and marriage. We'd invite all the women in our church to attend this three-hour event, and I would be the emcee. I learned so much from the women who taught these workshops. Though many women attended each time, I thought, *This ultimately is benefiting me!* I needed Titus 2 women speaking into my life, and all the hard work of finding a team to help me with food, name tags, the sound board, and decorating was well worth it. I loved our times together in meaningful community.

Dear reader, you do not have to journey alone in your Christian walk. Do not be afraid to take the initiative, try new things, and create new ideas! I have been blessed tenfold by my efforts to seek out women to study the Bible with me, to be my mentor, or to speak into my life as a Titus 2 woman.

GOOD MORNING GIRLS

After several years of leading women's Bible studies, the mentorship ministry, and Titus 2 Workshops, I began to struggle in my walk with the Lord. I now had two children, and life seemed to be moving at a very swift pace. I walked into the room where ladies had gathered for our fall Bible study, and I shared honestly with them my struggles. I told them how I desperately needed accountability and invited them to join a "6 a.m. Club." Eleven women signed up. The plan was for everyone to e-mail each other right at 6 a.m. to say we were awake and having our quiet times.

This worked for a while. But then reality hit, with nursing babies, wet beds, and fevers. Early morning was not going to work for everyone. So as our winter session began, our number in the group fizzled to five.

It was time for a new name, and we chose "Good Morning Girls." We gave one another grace in our accountability group as we made it our goal to e-mail the group sometime during the morning hours, and if for some reason we didn't e-mail, then afternoons and evenings were just fine too!

Two years later I shared about my Good Morning Girls group on my blog, and a woman commented. She told me how she had copied the idea and started her own Good Morning Girls group. A light-bulb went on. I had done a lot of organizing in my church to bring women together. What if I did this with Good Morning Girls groups online? I put a blog post together inviting women to join me and start their own groups. The response was overwhelming! I knew I could not run a ministry like this alone, so I phoned my high school best friend, Angela. She built the website GoodMorningGirls.org, and an online ministry was born.

> Two are better than one, because they have a good reward for their toil. For if they fall, one will lift up his fellow. But woe to him who is alone when he falls and has not another to lift him up! Again, if two lie together, they keep warm, but how can one keep warm alone? And though a man might prevail against one who is alone, two will withstand him—a threefold cord is not quickly broken. (Eccl. 4:9–12)

Within three years we had more than fifteen thousand Good Morning Girls from all around the world using Facebook groups, blogs, and e-mail to hold one another accountable in their walks with God. Women have formed their own groups with their friends from church, college, work, family, homeschool groups, or even old high school friends connecting across the country. Angela and I were awestruck when we saw military wives and pastors' wives and isolated homeschool moms finding one another on the message board and making new friends as they created small groups with like-minded women.

Once the groups were formed, women started asking us for Bible study advice. It was then that we decided to create an online Bible study for the GMGs! So Angela and I went to work creating free resources, like videos, devotionals, Bible reading plans, and study guides. We use the SOAP method that I shared in chapter 3 as our main study tool.

We have had the joy of leading women through the books of James, 1 John, Ephesians, and Colossians, as well as Proverbs 31. In the summertime, we do summer book clubs and other fun activities. At Christmastime, we pause for an Advent study.

God has done an Ephesians 3:20–21 with this little homegrown idea called Good Morning Girls.

> Now to him who is able to do far more abundantly than all that we ask or think, according to the power at work within us, to him be glory in the church and in Christ Jesus throughout all generations, forever and ever. Amen.

Do you need God to show up in your life? Do you need Him to do the unimaginable in your life? No one can study the Bible for you. You have to do this for yourself. You have to show up each morning and experience the wonder of God's amazing Word poured out before you. Drink of His living water and live well!

You do not have to walk this road alone. Together we are stronger! Look inside your church for Bible studies to join. Ask an older woman to mentor you. Start a Titus 2 Workshop, or go online and join a Good Morning Girls group. Let's lock arms together as sisters in Christ as we walk with the King!

How to Start a Good Morning Girls Group

1. Find a group of friends to form an online accountability group.
   • Women in your Sunday school class or church
   • Friends from your women's Bible study

- Past college roommates
- Relatives
- Neighbors
- Coworkers
- Other moms that you do life with

Still not sure who to invite? Then visit our online message board at GoodMorningGirls.org and find a group there to join! GMG groups are forming based on location, age of children, and roles—pastors' wives, homeschool moms, public school moms, working moms, stay-at-home moms, special-needs moms, etc. If you don't see a group that interests you, form your own online!

2. Once you know who is in your group, decide how you want to daily communicate with one another.
   - Facebook—set up a private group
   - Twitter—our hashtag is #GoodMorningGirls
   - E-mail
   - Text messaging
   - Skype

3. Sign up and subscribe to our blog at GoodMorningGirls .org, and don't forget to "like" us on Facebook.

You are now a part of a community that is going deeper with God. You will receive free e-mails, videos, e-books, Bible reading plans, and extra resources to help you in your walk with God.

Part 2

YOUR MARRIAGE

Then the Lord God said, "It is not good that the man
should be alone; I will make him a helper fit for him."

—Genesis 2:18

I n the world of reality television and reality blogging, we can miss
the reality of God's truth. The reality is we are sinners who married sinners, and that reality makes marriage hard. In the world of
images, the image of biblical marriages has been severely distorted.
Together, let's make Scripture a springboard for our actions and
reactions in marriage.

6

THE TIME-WARP WIFE

*If a man feels disrespected, he is going to feel unloved.
And what that translates to is this: If you want to love
your man in the way he needs to be loved, then you
need to ensure that he feels your respect most of all.*

—SHAUNTI FELDHAHN, *FOR WOMEN ONLY*

K eith and I met at church when I was seventeen and he was a
year older. He went to a Christian school, but his family did
not attend church regularly. I went to a public school, but my family
never missed a Sunday at church. And so our two opposite worlds
collided. It was not fireworks immediately, as I had very high standards and knew exactly what I was looking for in my future husband.
He made a fatal error on our first date.

He held my hand during the movie! That crossed the line with
me, and I came home and told my mom, "Nope, that is not the man
for me! He's too fast!" But we went on a second date. At the end of
the evening, as Keith was about to walk me to the door, I said, "I
am not interested in a physical relationship, so if you are looking for
that, you won't find it here." I jumped out of the car and ran into the
house. Luckily, my husband is a man who embraces a challenge, and
that day I became one. He pursued me while respecting my wishes,

and so began the uniting of two souls as we fell in love and became best friends.

We attended prom together, had a dreamy summer, and then went off to college. I went to Chicago to attend Moody Bible Institute, and he went to Columbus to attend Ohio State University. For four years, we maintained our long-distance relationship through letter writing (this was before cell phones and e-mail). Remember how I mentioned my husband loves a challenge? Well, dating long-distance is indeed a challenge. He wrote me a letter *every single day* for *four* years of college! And every evening I wrote him a letter, and then on the way to class in the morning, I dropped it in the mailbox. I now have boxes and boxes and boxes of letters. I'm guessing there are at least one thousand letters between the two of us we have saved!

Our summers were filled with dates, and our winter breaks were filled with time together. We would reconnect during quick weekend visits, and then it would end with me in tears, having to leave the man I loved so deeply. The years were hard and long, but we grew up together through this hardship, and finally college graduation came. Our years of long-distance dating taught us about the importance of communication, trust, loyalty, patience, praying for each other, and leaning on Christ first to meet all our needs.

The lost art of communicating through the written word was mastered in our dating relationship, and I believe it built a strong foundation for our marriage. Keith's and my ability to communicate our thoughts openly and listen lovingly to each other has been our greatest strength in marriage.

Fast-forward over a decade to the *Rachael Ray Show* when I was being featured as an example of a "time-warp wife." A video played of me serving my husband dinner and doing the laundry. A voice-over said, "These time-warp wives are still living in the fifties and loving every minute of it. Could turning back time improve your marriage?"

After the show aired, I got a lot of negative e-mails. I was called an airhead, a doormat, a Stepford wife, and the list goes on. But there was one woman in particular I remember commenting on the show. She was furious that I encouraged women to serve their families. She said, "You are taking women back two hundred years!" I thought, *Actually, I want to take women back two thousand years to God's Word.*

You see, the world was seeing a Christian marriage, and it looks different from the world's marriages. This caused viewers to bristle and question what they were seeing.

The Husband Is the Leader

For the husband is the head of the wife even as Christ is the head of the church, his body, and is himself its Savior.

—Ephesians 5:23

God has given us clear direction in the Bible that the husband is to be the leader of the home. Because each man is unique, that means each of our homes will be unique. Our leaders are all going to lead differently. My husband runs two businesses, so he works long hours. When he comes in the door, he is exhausted. He needs a warm meal, a cold drink, and some love! I do not ask him to do dishes because he needs to decompress from the stress of his work. But he always takes time to go outside and play with the kids or sit and listen to us all share our ups and downs of the day.

After fifteen years of marriage and conflicts and long talks sometimes involving tears, I have learned his likes and dislikes, and he has learned mine. As a result, we are able to keep each other quite happy, and we rarely argue over the small stuff anymore.

What are your husband's likes and dislikes? Mine likes heavy starch on his shirts, an endless supply of water bottles, and iced tea. Maybe yours likes meat and potatoes for dinner, cans of Coke in the fridge, and a clean sink. Maybe he couldn't care less about any of that, and he happily makes his own meat and potatoes, cleans his own sink, and buys his own Coke. Wonderful! Some husbands like to help their wives with the laundry or cooking. Many husbands like to show their love in this way. My husband and I have chosen to take traditional roles in the home. This works for us.

The biblical principles we apply to our marriages should be the same, but how this is carried out in our homes will look different. There are no cookie-cutter marriages. Your husband is not my husband, but my God is your God, so our principles should match!

BIBLICAL PRINCIPLES FOR MARRIAGE

- God created wives to be helpers to our husbands (Gen. 2:18).
- God commands wives to respect our husbands (Eph. 5:33).
- God commissions our husbands to be leaders of the home (Eph. 5:22–24).

YOU ARE YOUR HUSBAND'S HELPER

You are your husband's helper. That's a hard statement to swallow for today's liberated woman! Genesis 2:18 says that when God created Eve, she was created to be a "helper fit for him [Adam]." That is one of the wife's purposes. When you act as a "helper fit for [insert your husband's name here]," you are glorifying God. You were created to be your husband's helper, yet this is a tough thing for a modern woman to accept.

It is hard for women to sit back and simply assist their husbands. We are tempted to lead them, boss them, and criticize them. Often we expect them to take care of themselves and us, be tidy, and help us. But in actuality they are not our helpers. We are their helpers. God desires that they be servant leaders, but whether they are actually doing that should make no difference as to our attitude of being their helpers.

Here's an important point: you were not created to be a helper to *all* men. Women are not beneath men. Some women work in the workplace for men. They are paid to assist those for whom they work. Our culture has no trouble with this concept. But within the home, there appears to be a struggle. Women feel they are placing themselves beneath a man when they choose to help their husbands. I wonder: why is it noble to help men in the workplace, help orphans, help widows, help your pastor, help the neighbors, or help your parents, but degrading to help your husband—your groom, your lover, and your best friend?

I remember a time in our marriage when I was assisting one of our pastors with a vacation Bible school curriculum. Every time he called, I did what he asked. Then my husband asked me to help with some files, and I let the project sit for weeks. My husband came to me and said, "Why is it you will so willingly help the pastor, but the files still sit there? I feel if the pastor called right now and said, 'Can you help me with some filing?' you'd be there in a heartbeat to do it for him. But when I ask, you are slow to respond."

He was right! I had my priorities mixed up.

Helping our husbands is meant to be a beautiful blessing to our marriages and fulfilling to wives. Many women are missing out on this blessing. Here's the key: you were created specifically to be the helper of your man. So what your husband needs will differ from what my husband needs. My husband needs me to iron his shirts. Your husband may enjoy ironing. Your husband may like your children to have an early bedtime so he can spend time with you alone, while my husband may want a late bedtime for the children so he can spend quality time with them. Neither is right or wrong, but it does look different in application.

THREE WAYS YOU CAN BE A
HELPER TO YOUR HUSBAND

- *Know your husband.* Know his likes and dislikes, and help him in the areas he has asked for help. Do not wait for him to make a list or ask you to do something, but always have an attitude of helpfulness with eyes wide open looking for ways to meet his needs.
- *Do not compare your husband to your friend's husband, your brother-in-law, or even your pastor!* Your husband is unique, and you are unique; therefore, you have a unique marriage. You must seek to please your husband and no one else.
- *Do not wait for your husband to "deserve" to be helped.* You should do what is right no matter what others are doing around you.

CONSIDER YOUR HUSBAND'S NEEDS

How can we practically put our husbands' needs for help above the needs of our children, home, and ministry?

Consider this scenario: A woman invites over a couple of families for dinner. She has been cooking and cleaning all day, and by the time the guests arrive, she is nearly exhausted, but she has a second wind from all the excitement.

She wants to be a good hostess, so as people take a seat in the living room, she begins to offer drinks. She gets some drinks for the children. She pours some drinks for her friends, and as she serves it to them, her husband asks, "Honey, can I have an iced tea?" She thinks, *What? I'm working hard here in the kitchen while you sit there on the couch, visiting, and you have the audacity to ask me for a drink?* So in front of everyone she answers, "You have two feet; get it yourself." Everyone laughs, including her husband (he's so embarrassed, what choice does he have?). He gets himself a drink, helps her in the kitchen because he realizes she's stressed, and the night goes on. She thinks, *It worked! He got the point and started helping!*

What happened there? Who came first in this scenario? The children and the friends. And her husband? Dead last. Worse, she humiliated him when it would have only taken a few more seconds to pour him a drink.

If she truly needed help, what could she have done? She could have asked, "Could you come with me into the kitchen for a second?" Once they were alone in the kitchen, she could privately say, "I need help; I'm feeling overwhelmed."

Opportunities to make our husbands a priority present themselves every day. Here are some practical ways I try to show my husband that helping him comes first:

1. When I am going to the store, I ask him if there's anything he needs while I am there.
2. When I make the grocery list, I consider what his favorite meals are (not just the children's) and be sure to make them.
3. When I bake a dessert or dish to take to a gathering with only women, he gets the first serving. (So if you see a hole cut out of a cake I bring, you'll know why!)
4. At gatherings, I usually get his drink for him. At home I offer him drinks regularly too. It's a gesture I enjoy extending to him to show my love.
5. I respect his thoughts and opinions above anyone else's.

In Proverbs 31:28, we see the husband of the Proverbs 31 woman rising up and praising his wife. Does your husband rise up and praise you? Could it be that he does not because he doesn't feel he is your first priority?

While praise from our husbands is nice, we should not serve our husbands just to receive praise from them, but also to please God. God created you and your husband to be "one flesh" (Matt. 19:5). Your relationship should be a priority above all others! We should ask ourselves, do we seek praise more from our friends and coworkers or from our husbands? Your husband's opinion should matter most. When we don't fight our nature and what God has created us for, we will find peace and blessing even in the midst of a difficult marriage, and we may find a difficult marriage blossom into a warm and loving marriage when we focus on being who God has created us to be rather than focusing on changing our husbands. Don't give your husband your leftovers; give him the best of you. And consider delivering him a refreshing drink with a kiss tonight!

GIVE YOUR HUSBAND RESPECT

Ephesians 5:33 says, "Let the wife see that she respects her husband."

When I was dating Keith, I had a strong desire to please him. I highly respected his opinion on everything. But about a year into our marriage, my respect for him started to slip. Those lingering moments when I looked deeply into his starry eyes began to fade with the reality of bills, stress, and disagreements.

We can't keep the butterfly feelings alive forever in marriage. That's not realistic. However, we mustn't let our respect for our husbands slip. Remember, your husband got on one knee and proposed because he liked how *you* made him feel. Most likely, you made him feel like a good man, able to conquer the world with you at his side. Does he still feel that way?

Since God commands that wives respect their husbands, we must define what that means and realize how it plays out in our actions. The Greek word translated "respect" in Ephesians 5:33 is *phobeo*, which means "reverence or awe." It can also mean "honor and esteem."[1]

Respect is an attitude of heart that will be displayed by our actions.

RESPECT YOUR HUSBAND

Here are some ways to display the respect, esteem, and honor you have for your husband:

1. Respect his knowledge, opinions, and decisions.

2. Don't be a nag, criticize him, or assume the worst of his actions.

3. Watch for sarcastic and disrespectful teasing, rolling of eyes, or bitter attitudes.

4. Respect his desire to work, protect, provide, and lead. Tell him, "I respect your hard work. I feel more secure when you are here and protecting the family."

5. Respect his need for physical intimacy. Do not get frustrated with your husband in this area. God made men different from women. His lack of romance at times may be frustrating, but we must remember that men were created with testosterone . . . and his desire is literally for you, and he will continually pursue you in the bedroom. Aren't you thankful he's pursuing you and not another woman? Respect his faithful and loyal pursuit! Give him what he needs. Respect your man in the bedroom. This matters to him.

Dr. Emerson Eggerichs says, "No husband feels fond feelings of affection and love in his heart when he believes his wife has contempt for who he is as a human being. Ironically, the deepest need of the wife—to feel loved—is undermined by her disrespect."[2]

In the end, showing respect to our husbands is a choice we make in obedience to God. When we push our husbands away through disrespectful behavior, we are pushing the Lord away. Don't assume because your husband quietly accepts your joking or your leadership on decisions that he feels respected. He just may not have the heart to tell you the truth because he loves you so much. So let me tell you for him—he needs you to respect him.

When You Feel Your Husband Is Not Worthy of Respect

In Ephesians 5:33, we see that husbands are commanded to love their wives, and wives are commanded to respect their husbands. "Let each one of you love his wife as himself, and let the wife see that she respects her husband." It is very important to note that oftentimes in hot arguments, our husbands are feeling disrespected, while we are feeling very unloved. We long for them to lead us lovingly, and we believe, *If only he would love me, I would respect him.*

Sometimes we must be the ones to go first. Go first by giving your husband what he needs—respect.

All of us have areas in which we struggle to respect our husbands. For some, it may be in the area of parenting; for others it's a difference in goals, likes and dislikes, too much time spent on sports and hobbies, mother-in-law troubles, or his lack of helpfulness around the house. And this is just to name a few; there are many other serious issues and addictions that require intervention.

None of us is married to a perfect man. All husbands are flawed, just as we wives are all flawed, simply because we are all sinners. In most sitcoms, the husband is the brunt of jokes. He is stupid, while the wife knows it all and runs the house. This may be culturally acceptable, but it is not acceptable to God.

God has placed an order in our homes according to Ephesians 5, and the man is the head of the home and is to be respected in that role. "The husband is the head of the wife even as Christ is the head of the church" (v. 23).

Since this order is God ordained, when a wife bucks the system and disrespects her husband, her problem is not with her husband but with God. Does she trust God enough to take care of her? Is she willing to quietly pray about the problem she is having with her husband and give God room to work in her husband's heart? Is she willing to support her husband fully as his helpmate and make it safe for him to make a mistake and ask for help, or does he fear his wife's harsh tongue when he fails and therefore does not feel safe to ask for help?

Oftentimes we disrespect our husbands out of selfishness. We are not getting our way or what we want, so we go the route of criticizing, crying, or pouting. You see, we as women think it is okay to cry in a fight but it is not okay for the man to get angry. We think he's not controlling himself and judge him for it. But why is it that women tend to cry and men tend to get angry? Because crying is often the result of a woman feeling unloved, and anger is often the result of a man feeling disrespected. We provoke our husbands' anger when we are disrespectful.

If you are not able to communicate respectfully with your husband about a concern, then wait to communicate with him about it. This takes patience, prayer, and emotional maturity. Otherwise, your husband will feel the need to pull back from you and disconnect. Then you will cry and tell him how unloved you feel. In reality, you have poked him in the eye, and now you are crying and begging him to see you and your pain. But he won't be able to see past his own pain.

When we are faced with our husbands' weaknesses, much about our maturity is revealed. Our husbands should not have to earn our respect, just as we would not want them to make us earn their love. Our spiritual maturity and emotional maturity are tested.

So if you have failed to be respectful, go and make things right with God and then your husband. Apologize and begin your journey toward doing what is right. You will need to trust in God to give you the strength to bite your tongue—until it hurts if you must—as you wrestle with self-control! In time, you will find an overwhelming sense of peace that the Holy Spirit will bring you as you walk yielded to the Spirit. (Regarding more serious matters, such as infidelity and addictions, I strongly suggest you talk to a trusted older woman, pastor, or counselor.) So I encourage you today, go and give your husband what he so desperately needs—respect—and in time, your marriage will bloom.

LETTING OUR HUSBANDS LEAD

I remember playing Monopoly Junior with my children when they were little. It wasn't long before they were going too many spaces ahead, having trouble counting the money, and starting to make up their own rules. As a result, we had some chaos. I pulled out and read the rules, they obeyed, and then we were able to enjoy the game.

Marriage today has become like a Monopoly game with no rules. Everyone is doing their own thing, and the end result is chaos, fighting, and divorce.

Ephesians 5:22 says, "Wives, submit to your own husbands, as to the Lord." Here we find God's order for the home. We have already talked about how our husbands are the leaders of the home, but this verse takes that one step further by commanding wives to submit to their husbands. Submission is a heart attitude that will be displayed in our actions. We humbly allow our husbands to take the lead. When we allow the husband to take the lead, friction and chaos within marriage are resolved because this is the God-ordained order for marriage.

Am I saying this is easy to live out in marriage? Not at all! Let me share a story with you.

After two years of homeschooling plus a move to a new school district, my husband decided it was time for my son to go to public school. I am not against parents making this choice for their children, but it was unexpected and not how I had planned the next year of our lives. I cried buckets of tears. We fought, and it was a pretty ugly fight. I said things I regret that I later apologized for. And as I saw that he was not budging, I calmed down and submitted. I visited the school and enrolled our son. The school was very nice and had high academic awards. We all began preparing mentally for the change our family was about to face. My daughter would remain homeschooled while my son attended public school, but I had a mix of emotions from anger to sadness. I wanted to do what was right. I wanted to honor my husband's decision. So I put my emotions to prayer.

Then some minor things happened that brought the conversation of homeschooling back up again. I did not want to cry and manipulate my husband to get what I wanted, but I was open in our conversation about my feelings, which had not changed. He said, "Homeschool him if that's what you really want." I sensed he was annoyed that I had not come around to sharing his same heart desires, so I said, "No, we have him enrolled in public school, and I respect your decision, so let's give it a try."

Another month passed, and I was invited to speak at a rather large homeschool convention. This was ironic since my son was about to go to public school! Before I brought this opportunity before my husband, I prayed once again with a heart submitted to my husband's lead but also in hopes that maybe, just maybe, God had changed my husband's heart. The conversation about public school began again; I gingerly navigated my way into our discussion, and this time was different. By this point, my son had voiced his desire to remain homeschooled, and God had changed my husband's heart. I was at peace about submitting to my husband, but my husband had come to a place where he believed it was better to keep my son home! I thanked God for answered prayer, unenrolled my son from public school, and began ordering homeschool curriculum for him.

It was a bumpy season during this time in our marriage, but I found that God's Word and principles are true. We must let our husbands take the lead, even when we don't agree with them. Had my husband not changed his mind, I would have gone forward in faith and sent my son to public school. But in this specific situation, I believe it was the very act of submitting willingly to my husband's desires and putting the situation to prayer that brought about a change of my husband's heart. What peace I had knowing that God changed his mind, and not his nagging wife!

My friend Karen Ehman likens this give-and-take communication process in marriage to dancing:

Ballroom dancing, when done by experts, can be beautiful to watch. The dancers swirl and twirl, sway and dip as they appear to glide effortlessly across the wood floor floating in perfect unison. At times the dance travels toward the girl. Then the direction changes, and it migrates back to the man's side of the floor. No matter the direction the couple moves, one thing is certain.

For the dance to fall into place, the woman must follow the man's lead.

It doesn't mean she's inferior or less than or subservient. It isn't about importance. It's about function and roles. If the end result—a smooth and breathtaking dance—is desired, there are no two ways around it: the gal must follow her partner's lead.[3]

WHAT ABOUT ABUSE AND AFFAIRS WITHIN MARRIAGE?

Marriage was created to be a gift. In God's design according to Ephesians 5:25, the woman is to be loved by her husband "as Christ loved the church and gave himself up for her." She is to be protected by her husband. Husbands are commanded to "love their wives as their own bodies" (v. 28). And they are to be faithful to them, as they are united together in one flesh.

But some husbands have gone astray. If you are in an abusive marriage, I encourage you to seek outside help from a pastor, a trusted friend, or a godly counselor. Break the silence. I know this will take great courage, but if you are in danger, make a plan to get you and your children to safety immediately. You will need the help of trusted friends or a women's shelter. The law is on your side—use it: file a police report, get a restraining order, and separate from your husband until he gets help.

God is for marriages! "'I hate divorce,' says the LORD, the God of Israel" (Mal. 2:16 NIV, note). Even a broken marriage can be restored and redeemed by the hand of God. But in the case of an affair, Jesus says in Matthew 19:9, "And I say to you: whoever divorces his wife, *except for sexual immorality,* and marries another, commits adultery." Many scholars believe infidelity is a biblical exception for divorce. Jesus does not say you *must* divorce an unfaithful spouse, but He says you *may.*

Dear reader, if you are in one of these situations, my heart is heavy for you. I have barely scratched the surface of these very difficult scenarios. This is hard for me to write because I know that each case is so unique, and I write in such broad terms. That is why it is imperative that you seek out someone in your personal life for help. If you have no one you trust, consider calling Focus on the Family's hotline at 1-800-A-Family (232-6459). Their Christian counselors are trained, and they will be able to listen to the details of your specific situation and guide you. Please get help today. There is hope.

BEING A TIME-WARP WIFE

Perhaps you don't wear a dress and a ruffled apron as you make dinner from scratch in a 1950s sort of way, but we are all called to be time-warp wives—to go back into time to the days of Scripture, where we find God's holy design for what marriage should look like. To a modern woman of today's culture, Christian marriages may look as though they are caught in a time warp. We cannot expect those who do not believe in God's Word to understand. But marriages are in jeopardy. Christian marriages need to be a light to the world! When we follow God's plan for marriage, we will be different, and our light will shine for the whole world to see. Go let your light shine, and keep walking with the King.

7

MARRIAGE IN THE AGE OF MEDIA

*One reason we struggle with insecurity: we're comparing
our behind-the-scenes to everyone else's highlight reel.*

—Steven Furtick

I remember the days before kids. Keith would come home from work, and we'd cuddle on the couch and talk, laugh, watch television, and sometimes fall asleep that way. Then he brought his first laptop home from work, and the *tap, tap, tapping* began. He would sit beside me on the couch and *tap, tap, tap* away. I grew to hate the sound his fingers made on the keys . . . that *tap, tap, tap* was like fingernails on a chalkboard to me. Why? Because the laptop was competing with me for my husband's attention!

Then came the BlackBerry a year later. The BlackBerry was an effective tool because it enabled my husband to get all his e-mail at his fingertips at all times. However, other guys warned my husband that the BlackBerry was a highly addictive device! It, too, became an annoyance to me. It seemed the phone was everywhere. It rang at the dinner table, in the middle of the night, in church, in the car while we were driving, and during family events. Now I was competing with a laptop *and* a BlackBerry!

About that time, we took an amazing vacation to Hilton Head, South Carolina. We left our son with my parents to get away and enjoy each other, but the BlackBerry came with him. He spent quite a bit of time on it, so I decided one day at lunch to take his picture since it was becoming a memory! In the first picture there were two sandwiches, and in the second, only one. I ate alone. Did we fight like cats and dogs over this problem? No. Not yet. Not until this happened:

Our world changed when I got a laptop (and later an iPhone). Now we could sit beside each other on our laptops! The tapping no longer bothered me because I was tapping too. I entered the world of blogging, Facebook, Twitter, YouTube, and Pinterest. I loved all the connections, and the sky was the limit to my learning; from recipes to decorating, from theology to motherhood—the Web world fascinated me!

Then the bottom fell out.

Technology began to be a main source of contention in our marriage. My husband would feel I was on the computer too much, and I could easily bring up his past to justify my time online and win the argument. But really we were both losing: losing our intimate connection with each other to the computer. Time and time again we would have to revisit this problem, until finally, late one night after tension, terrible words, and tears, we both surrendered. We simply had to make a change. We could not live another day like this. We loved each other and God too much to continue this path—but how would we change?

We had each developed habits that seemed impossible to break. It was hard for me to even remember the days when the only media source we had in our apartment as newlyweds was the television! And it was hard to navigate this area of our lives because there were no role models on how to manage these things. I couldn't say, "Well, my mom and dad did it this way," because they didn't have this technology.

So I did two things to resolve our issue. I began logging my hours online in a notebook so I could see where all my time was going. Then

I moved my laptop from where it was too easily accessible to another room. Having the computer off my beaten path kept me from hopping on when I was bored and then letting time slip away from me. In the same way, my husband began shutting down his work during evening hours and letting phone calls go to voice mail during meals. We also set aside one technology free evening a week that we spend together after the kids are in bed. We came to a place of peace because we listened to each other in love and respect, and we were proactive.

Has your husband suggested you spend less time online or watching television? I encourage you to listen and respect his desires. It will save you from a world of coming pain.

Marriage and Media Land Mines

I believe that technology is amoral. In and of itself it is neither good nor evil, but rather the way you use technology, especially in marriage, determines its morality. I have benefited greatly spiritually from all the media resources I use daily, but I've compiled a list of pitfalls that I see for marriage and media:

Time

We must be aware of how much time we spend online versus making sure our husbands' needs are met. It is easy for time to slip away online, so it's important to be proactive. Decide in advance how much time you will spend online. Set your cell phone alarm to go off when that time is up. When it goes off, be disciplined and move on. Especially in the evening, when you could be enjoying time in the bedroom meeting your husband's needs—just sayin'!

Inappropriate Relationships Online

> The devil prowls around like a roaring
> lion, seeking someone to devour.
>
> —1 Peter 5:8

I read recently that more than one-third of divorces in the UK now cite the use of Facebook and status updates as one of the reasons for their divorce.[1] Usually it led to an affair. Though my marriage is strong, I want in no way to leave a cracked door for Satan, so (as I shared in chapter 4) I have chosen to delete all men, except relatives, from my friends list on Facebook. This is a personal conviction, and I'm not suggesting all women should do this; but if you are currently talking to an ex-boyfriend online or flirting with a man other than your husband, stop. Take whatever measure you must to break off any inappropriate relationships.

Disrespectful Talk About Husbands Online

"Will my genius husband ever learn to hang his towel up in the bathroom?" "I'm about ready to throw the video game system out the window. I hate that my husband plays it all night long." "Sure would be nice if my husband called to let me know he'd be in really, really late tonight."

When I see online remarks like this, I cringe. We must carefully choose our words when referencing our husbands online. The Internet is public, so we must be careful not to complain, criticize, or vent about our husbands for the whole world to see. I have shared details about my husband without his permission and upset him. Once I shared something I thought was funny that happened to him. Let's just say that he did *not* think it was funny! Oops! We live, and we learn, and we do better next time. It's important to listen to our husbands' feelings and respect them. Remember God's Word says, "Let the wife see that she respects her husband" (Eph. 5:33). Our talk about our husbands online should stand out and be different from the world's. No husband bashing; rather, use the platform to sing his praises!

Pornography

Sadly, the Internet has introduced pornography into many Christian homes. I have not experienced this in my marriage, but many women suffer in marriages in which their husbands use, or are even addicted to, pornography online. We must be vigilant to protect our sons and daughters from this devastating addiction. Some tools you could consider to help you protect your family are Safe Eyes, k9 browser and iPhone app, or CovenantEyes.com.

Discontent

We tend to look at our friends' status updates or pictures and grow jealous, discouraged, or discontent with our own lives. This is a serious problem that social media has created for women. While it is fabulous to connect, for a wife whose husband never takes her out to dinner, it can be painful to hear about other couples' date nights. It can create comparisons, which are poison to your marriage! We can wrongly believe that another husband is better than our own by comparing them spiritually, romantically, financially, or physically. All men are flawed (just as we are); all marriages are flawed.

REALITY TELEVISION

There are endless reality television shows that portray marriage in myriad ways. This has brought about a vast amount of confusion in our thinking about marriage.

First, there are the reality shows where the man is a Casanova. This "reality" show is really a soap opera, filled with men who say and do all the right things. As women watch these shows and compare them to their own realities, they are sadly disappointed with their own marriages.

Second, there are the reality shows where the women wear the pants. The woman is strong, independent, and if her husband does not cooperate with her whims, she throws a fit. She knows how to manipulate her husband to get what she wants, and he sheepishly grins and bears it.

Third, there are the reality shows where the women have a revolving door of husbands. When the wife gets tired of her husband or they hit a bump in their marriage, she leaves him and finds another man to start over with. The children from these different marriages are rarely seen.

Fourth, there are the reality shows where the women don't marry their lovers; they simply move in with them. Fearing divorce and losing money, they'd rather live with a man without commitment than marry him and take their chances on losing what they have in the bank.

Finally, there are reality shows where the wife is cheating on her husband or a single woman is sleeping with someone else's husband. These women shamelessly flaunt their lifestyles with no reference to the damage they cause from their decisions.

The reality is these shows affect our perception of true reality and how relationships work. There's a heavy fixation on the elements of excitement in marriage without showing the benefits of a stable, committed marriage. There's an unhealthy emphasis on selfishness, stubbornness, independence, criticalness, and unfaithfulness threaded throughout these shows, and sadly, these shows both mirror and lead our culture.

When we habitually take in these distorted views of marriage, these attitudes and beliefs can creep into our Christian marriages. We can begin to think that this is the norm, and these behaviors are acceptable. The reality is that marriage is hard work, and every marriage has its problems.

THE "GRASS IS GREENER" SYNDROME

Sometimes we are tempted to think the grass is greener in other marriages. We imagine that someone has something better than what we have, and we want it. We can't see the dirt from our angle. And possibly the grass is super green in the front yard, but in the backyard it's filled with dead spots that are hidden from acquaintances.

To be honest, the neighbors on both sides of us literally have greener grass. They both have in-ground sprinklers and spend time tending to their yards. Their yards look gorgeous. Ours, on the other hand, is burned by the sun. While it's been regularly mowed and fertilized, it's clear I have not spent any time putting sprinklers out to water it. Keith and I have laughed and said, "The only green part of our lawn is where the neighbors' sprinkler has sprayed over onto our yard!"

We could have exactly what the neighbors have if we would simply water our yard and tend to it!

My friend Karen Ehman, in her book *LET. IT. GO.*, says, "Ask any seasoned turf-grass specialist (I'm related to one), and he will tell you this truth. The grass actually has the best chance of turning out Kermit-the-Frog green when it's frequently fertilized and habitually hydrated, and when the pesky, deep-rooted, and often recurring weeds are intentionally pulled out. That's where you'll discover the softest, greenest, thickest grass of all."[2]

This same principle applies in marriage. Before we jump ship or sit in discontentment, I wonder if we watered and tended to our marriages if we could have the greener marriage!

How to Water Your Marriage

- *Accept the fact that all marriages are flawed.* As Dr. Gary Chapman says, "Conflicts are not a sign that you have married the wrong person. They simply affirm that you are human."[3]
- *Make your husband second priority only to God.* Flip-flop your priorities so your marriage is not coming in dead last, and you will find grass that looks burned start to grow green again.
- *Set aside a regular date night.* Spend some time just enjoying your husband. Hold hands, steal kisses, talk, and listen. Slow down and enjoy each other as you did during the dating days!
- *Smile at your husband.* A genuine smile is simple but irresistible.

> - *If your grass is looking brown in some spots, tend specifically to those spots with prayer.* Do not let it go dormant or die! If necessary, seek professional counseling to find ways to water the burned areas and help them grow again.
> - *Do not neglect your marriage and assume that it will grow all on its own.* Just as my brown grass is not going to turn green on its own, my marriage isn't going to flourish on its own. To stay healthy, your marriage needs your attention. Discipline yourself to tend to it.

Know that you are *not* alone! There are some busy seasons of life, where spots of the grass will start to die. Dora cups and Chuck E Cheese take the place of romantic dinners out. Enjoy your family moments at Chuck E Cheese, but remember *also* to tend to your marriage. Don't let it get shoved aside, because in a dozen or so more years, your Dora cup drinkers will be out of the house and it will be back to just you and your husband. Will your grass be green at that point, or dead?

The choice is yours.

DATE YOUR MATE

If this book were written for husbands, I'd say, "Men, take your wives out! Women need that face-to-face, eye-to-eye communication. As your wife drowns in diapers, laundry, and long to-do lists, a little reprieve with you will fill her love tank, give her strength to press on with her mundane tasks, and build intimacy in your marriage."

But I'm writing to wives, and I suspect the majority of us do not go out on regular date nights for a multitude of reasons: lack of money, difficulty finding a good babysitter, husband's not interested, kids' schedules interfere with finding/making time to go out, and the list goes on!

So how important is a date night to your marriage?
One blog commenter wrote:

I'm just wondering how often you and your husband date or how
often you suggest that couples with small children should date.
My husband and I just started once-a-month dating in the spring
of this year. Right now I feel overwhelmed with my ministry as a
mom and I want a little extra time to remember that I'm a Mrs.,
but I wonder if I shouldn't take more time away from our family time. I'm torn between taking another date night each month
and keeping as much all-of-us-together family time as possible.[4]

Oh, I love this question! It's so real. We really do wrestle with
these things in life, don't we? I've asked this question before and
have struggled with guilt at times when I was away with my husband.

First, *date night is not mentioned in the Bible.* Therefore, as a
disclaimer, you are about to simply read my opinions. We do see a passionate love in the Song of Songs that shows we should always enjoy
intimacy with our husbands and seek quiet moments together, but
I thoroughly believe with creativity this can be done in our homes.

Second, *date night is cultural.* Many people around the world can
barely put dinner on their tables, much less find a night to go out on
the town.

Third, *our grandmothers most likely would not have known the
term "date night" for married couples.* My own mother has told me
that when I was a kid, she and my dad took us kids everywhere
with them. When they got together with other couples, they always
included all the children. That was normal. And my parents have
been married for more than forty years!

Here's how I see it. A good marriage is like an ice-cream sundae.
The ice cream, hot fudge, and whipped cream are your love, respect,
communication, intimacy, communion with God, laughter, winks,
prayer, tender kisses hello, and daily forgiveness and faithfulness.

A date night is—you guessed it—the cherry on top! Must you

have a cherry on top of a sundae to have a great sundae? I suppose it's all in your perspective. Some women might focus on the lack of a cherry and completely miss out on the winks, tender kisses, intimacy, and myriad other things that go into a great marriage on a daily basis!

My husband and I go in and out of date night seasons. A few years back, we had a great college-aged babysitter who came steadily for a year and a half every other week. We made great memories during that time. But she moved on and life got busy with the kids' activities in the evening. Right now four evenings a week our kids have an activity outside the home. It just feels good to be home in the evening!

So we started a date night in our home. All summer long, on Saturday nights when the kids were in bed, we watched a video series on marriage together and then talked about it and enjoyed some meaningful time together.

It's the daily love of listening, forgiving, caring, respecting, and being sensitive to the other person that builds a great marriage. If you get to go out on a date night—*that's the cherry on top!*

Should you feel guilty for going out on a date night and leaving your children at home? Only you can answer that. How much time have you spent with them this week? With whom are you leaving them? Can you afford the things you do on date night? What does your husband think?

If you know your children are in a warm, loving environment and your husband wants to go—go for it! And thoroughly enjoy this blessing entirely guilt-free. God gave us good things to enjoy, and you should not feel guilty for enjoying alone time with your husband. Many marriage counselors recommend implementing a date night for couples who are struggling. This time away from the pressure of home can really strengthen communication and connection.

Is your marriage stale? Is there no way to get away for a date night? No problem! You can have your cherry on top at home. Here's how: Flirt again. Kiss again. Throw out your five-year-old pajamas and buy something new. Rent a movie and cuddle together. Take a shower together. Or set up a massage area in a candlelit room! A back rub to a husband is as flowers to a wife. Give him a long back rub with massage oils, and watch him open up to you! Make a pie, light a candle, and sit down at the kitchen table and just talk together. Take a book to the couch or bed, and cuddle and read together as a couple. Song of Songs 1:2 says, "Let him kiss me with the kisses of his mouth! For your love is better than wine."

This is the type of marriage your children *need* to see! Four different times I have been contacted by production companies who would like to film my marriage for a documentary or reality show. We have turned them down for various reasons, but let me testify to this: reality television stuff can't hold a candle to a real marriage that is built on the foundation of God's Word and is built up in passionate love and respect.

So grab your husband's hand, make your marriage a priority, and walk with the King!

8

BANISHING BITTERNESS TO FIND HAPPILY EVER AFTER

As the wife sees her husband's goodwill and forgives the past, many of her disrespectful feelings can leave her. Even if some remain, her respectful actions can empower her to influence the marriage in the direction she longs for it to go.

—EMERSON EGGERICHS, *LOVE AND RESPECT*

The day I found out I was having a little girl, I began dreaming of tutus and frilly dresses. I was so excited to dress up my little girl in ribbons and bows. I purchased princess movies at garage sales and scouted out sales on princess dresses. Little did I know that my daughter would come along and dislike anything with the word *princess* on it! She had zero interest in the movies and rarely dressed up in her princess dresses.

From time to time, she would wear one to a princess party, and it was fun for the day, but she never fully got into the imagination side of it. I, on the other hand, always loved the idea of happily-ever-after endings. As a little girl, I dreamed of marrying a man who would sweep me off my feet—never did I imagine that I might fail to act "princess-like"!

THE CRITICAL, CRANKY WIFE

Sometimes I can be cranky, especially when my husband parents differently than I do. For example, I like an early bedtime for the kids, but recently my husband has been allowing the children to stay up late—much too late for my patience! And when I get cranky, I get critical.

It's easy for me to slip into the roles of teacher and judge to my husband. I think as wives, we see our husbands' faults and point them out—but does taking that role ever bring a woman marital bliss? Nope!

We know that when our husbands fell in love with us, it was *not* because we were wonderful critics, teachers, and judges.

They married us because they loved the sparkle in our eyes when we smiled at them.

They loved how we made them feel.

They loved how we respected their thoughts and wanted to hear and understand them.

They loved how we embraced their dreams of the future and were so trusting and loyal and how we overlooked their shortcomings.

Proverbs 19:13 says, "A wife's quarreling is a continual dripping of rain." Do you catch yourself maybe not criticizing your husband out loud but thinking critical thoughts in your heart? Maybe he comes home late from work one night and you're annoyed that dinner is cold. Then he does it again another night that week. Then he is tardy yet once more, and suddenly you boil over with anger and an abundance of bitterness comes out. Yeah, I've been there!

Luke 6:45 says, "The good person out of the good treasure of his heart produces good, and the evil person out of his evil treasure produces evil, *for out of the abundance of the heart his mouth speaks.*"

What if, in the dinner situation, we thought how blessed we are to have such a hardworking husband who brings a paycheck home so we can have a warm home, food on the table, and a bright future for the children? There are moms who have no husband to expect at dinnertime. They are living paycheck to paycheck and are worried about their children's future. If we thought this way when our husbands walked through the door, they'd be greeted with a warm hug and a big kiss rather than the cold shoulder.

Who we are at home, behind closed doors, is who we really are.

Does your husband come home to a quarrelsome wife or a wife who has a sparkle in her smile when she looks at him?

Do our husbands feel judged by us, or do they love the way we make them feel?

Sometimes we need to have a talk with our husbands to air or resolve issues. But other times we need to choose to overlook their flaws and look at our own. The reality is that I can be a critical and cranky wife at times, and that is not acceptable. We need to resolve our own heart issues and choose to have joy because joy does not come from our husbands but from God.

Why There Is Conflict in Marriage

We don't have to look far to detect the reason for conflict in marriage. Simply look at any toy store's Christmas catalog! The section for boys is filled with Matchbox cars, swords, dinosaurs, planes, and trains. The section for girls is filled with Barbies, baby dolls, sparkle nail polish, princesses, and ponies.

From birth, boys and girls are clearly different! And they grow up into men and women who are still very different.

Why is marriage difficult? Because God made men and women different! And when we come together and rub each other the wrong way, we can choose to respect and love each other's differences or we can choose to fight.

How we handle conflict will determine whether there is peace, joy, and unity in our marriages, or contempt, bitterness, and isolation.

Disagreements and Maturity in Marriage

The first disagreement of our marriage came right after Keith and I made our vows. Literally. My husband and I had just lit our unity candle, and all eyes were on us as the music played. We could see our bridesmaids and groomsmen giggling, so we looked to see what was funny—and there was our unity candle, totally snuffed out.

We have on video me whispering, "Should we relight it?" then my husband answering, "No." Then I look at him very longingly as if to say, *Please, can we relight it?* and his facial expression clearly responds, *Sorry, but nope!* I followed his lead, which was to stand there holding hands and gazing into each other's eyes, smiling, while inside I really wanted to go light that candle!

Then on our honeymoon, we faced our second disagreement over what television show to watch. I can't remember what show he wanted, but I wanted to watch the Miss America Pageant! I watched it every year with my sisters growing up, so it seemed normal to invite him to watch it with me. He, on the other hand, was surprised that I even cared and promptly went to sleep! That hurt my feelings.

Looking back at the honeymoon scenario, I can see a lot of immaturity on my part. I dug my heels in over watching a silly television show that now I'd never invite him to watch. I'd like to believe that I've matured . . . but it wasn't long ago we had a tense moment over him not eating the eggs, toast, and oranges I had made him for breakfast because he was late for an appointment. I was not a happy camper. And he ended up eating them and being late. But then he was mad that I was mad . . . and, well, you know how it goes—all downhill from there.

Maturity could have helped in these situations if I'd remembered a few essentials:

1. *Unexpected things will come into your marriage.* No one could have predicted our unity candle would go out. When these unexpected scenarios arise, lovingly listen and respect your husband's wisdom. It will save you a lot of heartache. I'm glad I didn't bother trying to change his mind, because in reality he saved me from embarrassment!

2. *Sometimes fights are a result of our selfish expectations.* I expected my husband to act like my sisters on our honeymoon rather than like a guy. Maturity has helped me realize I married a *man,* and men are, well . . . men.
3. *Sometimes we fight because we don't get what we want.* James 4:1–2 says that fights often start because we want something and don't get it! Take the breakfast scenario. I wanted my husband to eat and appreciate my food. At first glance, that doesn't seem so awful of me. But due to my criticism, I got what I wanted. He ate the breakfast I prepared him, and then he was *late.* Twelve minutes late, to be exact—to his grandmother's funeral! (Don't details change everything in a story?)

Disagreements are inevitable in marriage. The key to overcoming the inevitable and maintaining emotional, spiritual, and physical intimacy is to be mature enough to recognize the areas where we were at fault and apologize.

Maturity means we learn from past mistakes and do it differently next time. Have you lost your cool and rambled on in anger and said things you regretted to your husband? Move on to maturity.

I quoted this earlier, but it bears repeating. Proverbs 10:19 says, "When words are many, transgression is not lacking, but whoever restrains his lips is prudent." Boy, do I wish I could master this one little verse, because I know it works wonders in my marriage when I hold my tongue!

I think of parenting and how I say to the kids, "Whoever is more mature will be the first to apologize." Isn't that what our heavenly Father says to us, His children? It's the more mature one who has the strength to apologize.

Defuse disagreements by being mature . . . hold your tongue, pray over your words, look to the interest of your husband, and remember that you are an extension of God's hand to your husband when you bless him.

TRIPLE TROUBLE IN MARRIAGE

Let's explore three common problems in marriage.

Disappointment with Unmet Expectations

False expectations can be formed while dating. As you try to win each other's hearts, both parties put their best foot forward and seek to please each other. The reality is, character qualities we did not see during the dating years will rear their ugly heads as new seasons of life bring new challenges. Does that mean we married the wrong person? No!

How we handle our husbands' shortcomings reveals more about our own character than our husbands'. Bitterness, resentment, harsh words, and a critical spirit are not character traits our husbands expected to see in their wives. The truth is, usually both parties change a bit in the way they selflessly love.

So what do you do? Let go of your expectations, remain steadfastly faithful to your marriage vows, and remember that you married a sinner who needs grace—the same grace Christ gave us at the cross. Look into his eyes, deep into his soul, and most likely there is a hurting man inside. He may be suffering from fear of failure, insecurity masked in a big ego, maybe wounds from childhood, and wounds from your marriage. Pray God brings a spiritual role model into his life. Disrespect rarely motivates a man. So try something new in your marriage. Sit down and write out five things you love about your husband. And then? Tell them to him!

Disappointment with Husband's Spiritual Leadership

This problem is a serious epidemic in Christian marriages. It is very hard for wives to respect and follow a man they are not trusting to lead them in God's ways. But disrespect is rarely a motivator for a husband.

Some women are married to men who are mature in Christ, who

had parents model for them what a spiritual leader looks like. Others married husbands who will not darken the door of the church. Still others of you have husbands who attend church every Sunday, but only if you wake them up to go. (He might keep sleeping if you didn't do all the work to get the family there!)

Sometimes as wives, we can create a mental checklist to evaluate our husbands' spirituality. It might look like this:

1. Does he sing loudly at church?
2. Does he initiate Bible time with the family?
3. Does he pray with me before we went to bed?
4. Does he act like that guy in my small group who seems to be a spiritual giant?
5. Does he read the Bible as often as I do?
6. Does he go to a men's Bible study group?
7. Does he express with words how much he loves Jesus, like I do?
8. Is he as giving with our money as I am?
9. Does he know as much about the Bible as I do?

And we come to the end of those questions and declare, "Nope! He is not all those things. Therefore my husband is not the spiritual leader of our home—I am."

While I do believe that many husbands are failing in their role as spiritual leaders, I want to encourage you not to go down this very dark path. It will not lead to a spiritually stronger husband. He will sense that you disrespect him in this area.

It seems so easy for us wives to criticize our husbands in this area. We have an ideal we want them to meet, and we fail to realize that the day they walked down the aisle, they became the heads of our homes. Ephesians 5:23 doesn't say the husband *ought* to be the head of the home; it says that by virtue of office he already is!

I hear so many women say, "He's not leading." The reality is that your husband is *always* leading. He may just be doing a lousy job.

And if he has abdicated his leadership to you, then he is still leading, but leading by abdication.

My husband is my leader in every area. He reads his Bible every morning, but his walk with God simply does not look like mine. We must recognize that a man's walk with God looks different from a woman's. Some men may be openly expressive in worship, but after more than three decades in church, I have seen this is the exception, not the rule.

God made our men strong and fierce to fight battles, slay enemies, and make bold moves for His kingdom. My husband's faith is unwavering. His integrity stellar. His courage to be a truth teller unstoppable. His knowledge of theology deep. But will he get flowery about his love for Jesus or anything else? Not likely.

His walk with God looks different from mine, just as your walk with God might look different from mine.

If you take nothing else from this, please hear me on this point: Leave room for your husband to mature in this area. Do not treat him as though he is less than you if he is not as spiritually strong. Think of the first day you held your first child in your arms. Were you a mature parent, ready to handle every issue you would face in parenting? What if your husband had a mental checklist, and you were not measuring up to his standards as a mom? You'd be devastated. If you need anyone's support as a mom, it's your husband's. In the same way, he needs your support in his role of leadership.

Give your husband room and time to mature. Pray for his leadership rather than criticize it. Take note when he does something right. Your husband is in a place of inescapable leadership. That is a tremendous burden to carry. Lighten his load, step back, and let your husband lead.

Letting Bitterness Fester

Sometimes our marriage problems are all in our heads. I'm not saying we're crazy, but I am saying our thought patterns affect our marriages. We can give respectful lip service and appear on the outside to be very respectful toward our husbands, but on the inside be eaten up with bitterness. Hebrews 12:15 warns, "See to it that no one fails to obtain the grace of God; that no 'root of bitterness' springs up and causes trouble, and by it many become defiled."

How to Banish Bitterness

- *Confess your bitterness.* Get alone in prayer, and confess your bitterness as sin to God.
- *Filter your thoughts.* Put a biblical filter on your thoughts. My personal filter is Philippians 4:8: "Finally, brothers, whatever is true, whatever is honorable, whatever is just, whatever is pure, whatever is lovely, whatever is commendable, if there is any excellence, if there is anything worthy of praise, think about these things." I use this verse to frisk all my thoughts about my husband at the door of my mind. When I have a thought about my husband, I ask myself, "Is this a noble thought? Is this pure? Is this lovely? Admirable? Praiseworthy?" If it is not, I must do what 2 Corinthians 10:5 says: "Take every thought captive to obey Christ." I must make my thoughts obedient to Christ.
- *Replace bitterness with thankfulness.* I do not let those thoughts swirl in my head because eventually everyone in the family can see it in my demeanor, my lack of joy, and even in my words. It can't be hidden. I have to replace those thoughts with thankful thoughts full of grace.

Whenever I start to feel critical or bitter toward my husband, I must choose instead to forgive my husband and to pray for him. I confess my sin of bitterness and ask the Lord to give me eyes to see my husband as He sees him.

If you are looking to overcome bitterness in your marriage,

realize that this is not something that will happen overnight. It's a lifelong journey of guarding your mind and your marriage. The enemy would *love* to get a foothold in your marriage using bitterness, so beware! Put Philippians 4:8 as a filter over your mind. Be free from bitterness!

FINDING FORGIVENESS

My children have a favorite tree they love to climb in our backyard, but last spring we found a massive vine of poison ivy crawling up the tree. Out of fear for my children's safety, I worked vigilantly to spray and remove all the poison ivy. I knew if they rubbed up against it, they would be in a lot of pain, and the tree would no longer be a pleasant place.

In the same way, I want to caution wives not to poison their marriages with their lack of forgiveness. If you continue to hold on to your hurts, a root of bitterness will grow inside of you. Over time this bitterness will poison your marriage. Scripture tells us, "Then Peter came up and said to him, 'Lord, how often will my brother sin against me, and I forgive him? As many as seven times?' Jesus said to him, 'I do not say to you seven times, but seventy times seven'" (Matt. 18:21–22).

Ruth Bell Graham says, "A good marriage is the union of two forgivers."

I don't know what your husband has done or said, but if you are holding on to it and refusing to forgive your husband, you are going to poison your thoughts and your heart. It is going to come out in different ways in your home, and soon your home is not going to be a pleasant place. There will be pain and suffering there.

I encourage you today to go to the foot of the cross and lay down all that pain and all that sorrow and exchange it for the grace and mercy that God gives. Give your husband forgiveness, the same forgiveness you experienced at the cross. If you have hurt your husband, seek his forgiveness. Once you remove this poison from your marriage, your home will be restored. You will be able to honor and respect your husband again. That is God's will. God is for strong marriages!

HAPPILY EVER AFTER

The days of dreaming of being a princess are long gone. I certainly found my Prince Charming, but my tiara came tumbling off when I realized marriage was hard work. Without the Word of God and the Holy Spirit's help, I'm not sure we would have made it very long! My husband and I have read countless books on marriage and have pursued building a strong marriage. As a result, my marriage far exceeds anything I could have ever dreamed. My tall, dark, handsome husband still lights my fire when he smiles at me! I have no fear for our future because following God's Word is a safeguard to our marriage. We will surely fall on hard times again and again, but together we can weather the storms life brings as we walk with the King.

9

THE "COMPLETING HIM" MARRIAGE CHALLENGE, WEEK 1

It is not your love that sustains the marriage, but from now on, the marriage that sustains your love.

—DIETRICH BONHOEFFER, QUOTED
IN *THIS MOMENTARY MARRIAGE*

G od created marriage in the garden of Eden. He created Adam and said it was not good for him to be alone. So He created Eve, who was a perfect complement to Adam. Then a marriage took place. God gave His daughter away.

In Genesis 2:24, God says, "A man shall leave his father and his mother and hold fast to his wife, and they shall become one flesh." We see that God created marriage. This is why Jesus says, "What therefore God has joined together, let not man separate" (Mark 10:9).

You are the perfect complement to your husband. You were not created to compete with your husband but to complete him. You have the power to breathe life into your marriage or to break it. Our culture has beaten men down and sent them mixed signals about who they should be as husbands. Our men need our encouragement. They need us to come alongside them and complete them.

So today we begin a ten-day marriage challenge that is about being intentional as we complete our husbands rather than compete with our husbands. Our husbands are each unique, so this challenge will be about discovering what it is *your* husband needs. Each of the ten days will include a verse, a thought, a challenge, and an application. Your husband is going to be blown away by your desire to please him over the next ten days! So buckle up, because you are about to go on a really fun ride! Together let's fine-tune how we can bless our husbands.

DAY 1—CAPTIVATE YOUR HUSBAND

Rejoice in the wife of your youth, a lovely deer, a graceful doe. Let her breasts fill you at all times with delight; be intoxicated always in her love.

—PROVERBS 5:18–19

Do you remember when you first started dating your husband? He saw you as beautiful and excellent. You fascinated him. Your eyes twinkled, you smiled with each thought of him, and you bonded over long conversations of who you both were and dreamed to be.

Do you remember the butterflies you felt when he was around, how it thrilled you when he held your hand, how your mind soared when you dreamed of taking his name as your last name? And then when he slipped the engagement ring on your finger, you stared at the reality that indeed you were about to become the wife of the man with whom you were head over heels in love!

Remembering does wonders for our souls to remind us of how fabulous our husbands truly are. We are the wives of our husbands' youth, and God tells our husbands to be satisfied, intoxicated, and captivated by our love.

But I wonder, are you still captivating him, or have pleasing, pursuing, touching, loving, listening, and feeding your relationship been lost somewhere in the busy shuffle of life?

Today's Challenge

Reflect on your dating days. In what ways can you and your husband regain some of what has been lost in the daily shuffle of life?

Purpose today to do something that reminds your husband of the new bride you once were. Maybe it's wearing something you know he loves on you (remember we dressed to please back in those dating days!), going somewhere you both used to enjoy going together alone, looking at photos together of your dating days, watching a favorite movie, or just simply sitting together, talking, listening, holding hands, rubbing his back, and paying attention to your amazing husband. Treasure him today!

Application

Write what you will do to captivate your husband today:

_____

_____

_____

_____

DAY 2—REMEMBER YOUR MARRIAGE VOWS

*[Jesus] answered, "Have you not read that he who created
them from the beginning made them male and female,
and said, 'Therefore a man shall leave his father and his
mother and hold fast to his wife, and the two shall become
one flesh'? So they are no longer two but one flesh. What
therefore God has joined together, let not man separate."*

—MATTHEW 19:4–6

Do you remember your marriage vows? If you did not write your own, then they probably went something like this:

> I, _____, take you, _____, for my lawful husband, to have and to hold, from this day forward, for better, for worse, for richer, for poorer, in sickness and in health, until death do us part.

"Until death do us part." Do you remember that line? Statistics say that in America, more than 50 percent of marriages do not last a lifetime.[1]

Do you take your vows seriously? God does. Malachi 2:14 says God is a witness to our marriage covenant. And Ephesians 5:22–33 says marriage is a picture of Christ and the church.

Let's agree with God that indeed our marriage vows are sacred and permanent. They acknowledge that we are more than just living together. We are committed. We are committed "until death do us part"!

Today's Challenge

Remember the day you made your sacred vows. If you have a copy of them, read them. Take some time to sit down and look at your wedding album or watch your videotape or DVD and invite your husband to look or watch with you. Remind yourself of your commitment to your husband—for better or worse.

Application

Write out a prayer asking God to help you keep your marriage vows:

_____

_____

_____

_____

_____

_____

Day 3—Pray for Your Husband

The prayer of a righteous person has
great power as it is working.

—James 5:16

Here's where the hard work begins! If you do not yet own *The Power of a Praying Wife* by Stormie Omartian, get it![2] It is an excellent guide and a treasure to keep on your bookshelf.

Prayer changes things. Do you believe that? Then let's get started! Here are some areas about which you can begin to pray for your husband: his wife (that's a good place to start, right?), his faith, his priorities, his parenting, his health, his work, and his future.

Like a string around your finger, reminding you of something important, let your wedding ring be a reminder to pray daily for your husband. I challenge you to pray every time you look down and see your wedding ring. When you take your ring off to wash dishes or shower, say a sentence prayer for your husband. When you are watching television, reading a book, or typing on your computer and your ring flashes your way, whisper a prayer for your husband. Make it a habit to pray for your husband.

I have always used symbols, such as my wedding ring, as reminders to pray for my husband throughout the day. Another symbol I use is a bucket truck. My husband is in the bucket truck industry. When the kids and I are driving, we regularly pass bucket trucks, and immediately I have one of the children say a sentence prayer for Daddy and his job. As we build these habits ourselves, we also train our children to follow our example.

Today's Challenge

Ask your husband if he has any specific prayer requests you can be praying about for him. Then set aside some time today to get alone with God and pour out your heart and prayers to God on behalf of your husband. Today, be your husband's prayer warrior. Tomorrow, be your husband's prayer warrior. Forever, be your husband's prayer warrior!

Application

Write out your husband's prayer request and also what symbol you will use as a reminder throughout the day to pray for your husband:

_____

_____

_____

_____

Day 4—Admire Your Husband

As you wish that others would do to you, do so to them.

—Luke 6:31

Pop quiz:

1. List all your husband's flaws.
2. List all the things you admire about your husband.

Now grade yourself: Which question was easier to answer?

There are some women out there who find it easier to admire their husbands than list their flaws (especially if they're newly-weds!). But I would venture to say that most of us find it easier to list our husbands' flaws. It's a part of our sin nature!

So let's break out of that mold. Let's go against the grain of the world and praise our husbands.

Here's what I admire about my husband:

1. *He is wildly intelligent.* He continually amazes me with his ideas, visions, and success.
2. *He is fiercely strong.* He has survived much adversity in his life and can handle heavy burdens and challenging situations with ease.
3. *He is quick-witted and hilarious!* He makes me laugh all the time. His perspective on life and happenings cracks me up.
4. *He makes the kids laugh.* He is a fun dad. Just two days ago, in the midst of being extremely sick with no voice, he was popping cherry pits out of his mouth by pulling his ear. The kids roared with laughter! He is a very fun, hands-on daddy.
5. *He is a patient listener.* He listens and listens and listens, and when I think I'm done but remember one more detail I want to share, he listens some more. I am very chatty, and he is an excellent listener. He is the same way with the children. Every bedtime that he is able, he sits on the bed with each child and talks with them about their day. These turn into thirty-minute conversations regularly. I love it!
6. *He is loyal, trustworthy, and dependable.* What he says he will do, he does. He is a great provider and a strong leader. He is extremely consistent.
7. *Under all his mighty warrior strength, he is tender.* He has a soft spot in his heart for me and for the children. He would move mountains for me if he could. There is nothing he won't do for us. His favorite thing to do with Alexis is paint her nails. And his favorite thing to do with Alex is play football or teach him martial arts moves.
8. *He loves Jesus.* He teaches the children about Jesus. He prays for us. He fasts with me when I have heavy burdens. And he can be found regularly in his office, reading his Bible in the mornings.
9. *He has a very generous heart.* I wish I could share with you all the times he has generously given, but he would

not be fond of that. But trust me: this man is a giver—
big time!

10. *He supports me in my ministry.* He encourages me to stand
strong. He wisely advises me on issues. He keeps me
focused. He shares my passion and is my sounding wall
regularly for what I write.

Keith is the perfect fit for me. I am a strong woman, and it takes
a very strong man to lead me. I am so thankful I married my warrior!
God has blessed us greatly, and I know much of the blessings come
because I have a man who is yielded to God and His Word. He does
not waver in his faithfulness to God or to me. And the security he
gives me in this is priceless.

Thank you for letting me gush for a moment about my husband.
This is my opportunity to publicly sing his praises. Now it's your
turn. Write out your list, and if there's any public way that you can
sing his praises—do it! He will love it.

Today's Challenge

Admire your husband. List ten things you admire about your husband, and then read it to him or give it to him in the form of a letter.

Showing your admiration to him is so important. You may *think*
he already knows the things you admire about him, but in reality, we
don't tell our husbands often enough how much we do. So take the
opportunity to do it today!

Application

**Write out your list of ten things you admire about your
husband here:**

_____

_____

_____

_____

_____

DAY 5—COMMUNICATE WITH YOUR HUSBAND ABOUT YOUR PRIORITIES

Her children rise up and call her blessed; her husband also, and he praises her: "Many women have done excellently, but you surpass them all."

—PROVERBS 31:28–29

Have you ever felt it's hard to please your husband? That getting the praise of the Proverbs 31 woman is out of reach? I get e-mails from wives saying they work and work and work, and their husbands just never seem to appreciate it. We women can fill our plates to the brim with work, children's needs, activities, and ministry, but it's important that we seek our husbands' opinions. They can easily get squeezed out of the equation when it comes to our time management.

About seven years ago, I learned about the Walgreens and Rite Aid rebate systems. I was so excited to get freebies every week that participating in every rebate became almost like a game for me. I created a coupon box and began following all the ads and going from store to store getting deals.

I remember one day after I had run myself ragged with my newborn baby and toddler in tow, getting all of the deals, I complained to my husband about how hard it was and how he should appreciate it.

He looked at me kind of surprised and said, "I never asked you to do this."

I said, "But I'm helping us save money. Isn't that important to you?"

He answered, "I appreciate the fact that you are being mindful of your spending, but I worry about your safety when you are out with the kids. I'd actually prefer you take your extra time and stay home and keep the house in order."

"Oh," I said, disappointed. "But I like getting rebates and clipping coupons."

"I'm not saying you can't do it. I'm just saying I'd appreciate it more if you organized a closet or something."

It was then I realized that some of the time I spent working hard, *I thought* my husband would really appreciate what I was doing, but he couldn't care less about it. I was neglecting other things he really cared about.

It's important that we take the time to communicate so we can avoid a fight, hurt feelings, and bitterness.

Different seasons of life will require different priorities. Different personalities will have different priorities. A social husband may prefer that his wife plan cookouts rather than clean out closets, while an outdoorsman would prefer that his wife work in the garden with him. Each marriage is going to look different based on the leadership of the husband.

A lot of quarrels can be kept at bay if we are willing to ask our husbands their preferences and then be mindful of them.

Today's Challenge

Make a list of five things you currently do, and ask your husband to prioritize them for you according to what is important to him. For example: a clean home, home-cooked dinner, coupon clipping, service at church, having friends over for dinner, watching/doing sports with him—and don't forget sex. Some of you may find it odd to ask your husband what his priorities would be for you, but it's important to communicate about these things.

Application

Write out your list of five things here, and then run them by your husband:

If you have completed these first five challenges, a big high five goes out to you! I just know that your husband is wondering, *What is up with her?* And even if he hasn't verbalized it yet, he likes it.

I remember the first time I led these challenges on my blog at WomenLivingWell.org. I sensed the enemy fighting back as I tried to bless my husband. I posted my list of things I admire about Keith on my blog on a Sunday night. Soon after it was published, Keith and I got into a disagreement, and I went to bed upset with him. It wasn't until Tuesday that I said, "Go check out the wonderful things I wrote about you on Sunday!" It was interesting timing and a great reality check for me. Am I willing to do the hard things in my marriage even when the road is bumpy? I'm so glad I pressed on with the next five challenges that are coming in chapter 10. Don't stop now—with the help of God, we can press on. Keep walking with the King!

10

THE "COMPLETING HIM" MARRIAGE CHALLENGE, WEEK 2

*The covenant involved in leaving mother and father
and holding fast to a spouse and becoming one flesh
is a portrayal of the covenant between Christ and
his church. Marriage exists ultimately to display the
covenant-keeping love between Christ and the church.*

—JOHN PIPER, *THIS MOMENTARY MARRIAGE*

John Piper explains in *This Momentary Marriage* the deeper mystery of marriage written about in Ephesians 5:32. Marriage is a momentary gift, and it is patterned after Christ's covenant commitment to His church.[1] This is what makes divorce so sorrowful in God's eyes; it misrepresents Christ's commitment to us. And this is what makes some sitcoms and reality shows so troublesome; they steal the magnificent meaning of marriage!

Human marriage is temporary. On our day of resurrection, our earthly marriages will vanish and we will forever experience the faithful love of God. Do our marriages reflect this truth? Can the world see this mystery reflected within our Christian marriages?

You see, this "Completing Him" marriage challenge is about so much more than just trying to be a good wife. Hour by hour we receive the love, forgiveness, and grace of God, and hour by hour we must extend the same love, forgiveness, and grace of God to our husbands. So let's press on into the challenging tasks ahead as we seek to complete our husbands to the glory of God!

DAY 6—COOK YOUR HUSBAND'S FAVORITE MEAL

Train the young women to love their husbands.

—TITUS 2:4

Why is it significant to cook your husband's favorite meal? Here are a few reasons:

1. Often, meal plans end up catering to what the children like. This is one time that we are going to take our husband's preferences above everyone else's—including our own!

2. On special occasions, like Father's Day and our husbands' birthdays, our husbands become the center of attention. This is our chance to make them a priority for no reason other than we love them. Wouldn't we appreciate it if they did this for us? Let's go first and make a special day just for our husbands. Get into it—maybe make it a surprise and get the children involved. Take an evening to shower your husband with kisses, hugs, and all his favorites. It's not good to spoil your children, but it is okay to spoil your husband!

3. Take this opportunity to display your love. Titus 2:3–4 says the older women are to teach the younger women to "love their husbands." Selfishness hinders love. Take the time to give thoughtful care to how you can exhibit love to your husband.

I am reminded of *The Five Love Languages,* by Gary Chapman. In his book, the premise is that we all experience love differently. Some need words of affirmation, while others need quality time, gifts, acts of service, or physical touch.[2]

As we go through these challenges, we will hit on each of these love languages. There are some husbands to whom this challenge is going to speak volumes of love. So let's get busy in the kitchen, ladies.

Today's Challenge

Make your husband a priority. Ask him what his favorite dinner, dessert, and drink are. Be sure to serve him all three, one night this week. Bonus: cook his favorite dishes all week long!

Application

What are you planning to cook this week? If you aren't sure of your husband's favorites, just ask him.

_____

_____

_____

Day 7—Follow Your Husband's Vision

For the husband is the head of the wife even
as Christ is the head of the church.

—Ephesians 5:23

It is hard for us to step back and let our husbands lead. The challenge this week is to *listen*. Listen to your husband's vision for your family. Then enter into his vision and share what you dream and envision. From there see where the differences may lie and flesh those out. In the places where you do not see eye to eye, let your husband lead.

Pray for him as he leads. Then trust God that he will protect you as you obey Ephesians 5:23 in allowing your husband to lead. Indeed, this is a challenge!

Seven years ago my husband and I went out on a date night. During the course of dinner, my husband pulled out his napkin and a pen and began to draw out some career path changes. I was mortified! They were nothing like the path we were currently on. I was comfy and cozy and liked his career choice. And in the blink of an eye, he was changing everything.

I could hear the passion in his voice and see the excitement in his eyes. My mind said, *Follow your husband wherever he leads you,* but my heart said, *He's asking too much of me!* I wrestled with some of his choices but allowed him to lead.

It was scary. I cried for about the first two months off and on. I cried to my friends, cried to my family, cried to my husband, and yes, even cried in front of the children. A lot in our life changed as a result of his vision for our family, and I had to sacrifice a few things.

Five years later, I have a husband who thanks me for putting all my faith and loyalty in his decisions. It was not easy to make the choices he made. Knowing that I got on the roller-coaster ride beside him and hung on tight meant so much to him. We grew closer as a couple, and as a result, we saw qualities exhibited in each other that we had not seen in the first nine years of our marriage.

I am so thankful that God gave me the strength to follow my husband's vision. I won't say that it was all rosy. We had some very hard moments. But I trusted that the God who gave this command would protect me through this. And I can testify that God was, is, and will always be faithful!

Today, listen to your husband. Talk with him about his plans, dreams, and vision for your family. Share yours in return. Don't let it become a debate. Close your mouth and simply listen. Imagine how you can help him reach those goals. Remember the truth that behind every great man is a great woman.

Today's Challenge

Ask your husband if he has a vision for your family. Where does he see your family in one year, five years, and ten years? Listen. Some husbands may have dreams and plans you've never imagined, while others will find this question very difficult. Simply listen. And then support your husband's vision.

Application

After your husband shares his vision, write some of it here:

_____

_____

_____

_____

DAY 8—R-E-S-P-E-C-T!

Let each one of you love his wife as himself, and
let the wife see that she respects her husband.

—EPHESIANS 5:33

This can be a difficult verse to apply because some women have husbands who are not doing the first half of this verse: their husbands are not loving them as themselves. But I want to encourage you to go first—follow this command and respect your husband.

God commands us wives to respect our husbands unconditionally. Our men are not Boy Scouts trying to earn badges of honor. God does not say to respect the husband who is "worthy" of respect. It is simply their position of *husband* that we are to respect.

Think of what men will do for honor. They will take bullets from an enemy. While everyone is running out of a burning building, men will run up twenty flights of stairs to save lives. They will shoot the bear to protect their family. They are just wired this way, and isn't it glorious that they are?

Sometimes we women joke about the male ego—but it truly is tender. Deep down there's insecurity, and they need to know that they are adequate, they are enough, and they are worthy of our respect.

Sometimes it's hard to know exactly what it is that makes our husbands feel disrespected. Sometimes the strangest comment I make will make my husband angry. I don't see it as disrespectful at all, and it baffles me, yet he is clearly offended. It has taken time for me to learn what it is that makes him feel disrespected. But I can tell you a few things that all men disdain:

1. The wife rolling her eyes at him.
2. Criticizing him.
3. Complaining to her mother or girlfriends about his flaws.
4. Not respecting his knowledge, opinions, or decisions.
5. Nagging him or assuming the worst in his actions.
6. Using sarcasm to communicate bitterness.
7. Disrespecting his work, protection, provision, or leadership.
8. Disrespecting his "manhood."

Today, work on weeding out disrespectful thoughts and attitudes and exchanging them for respectful ones. Remember, you respect your husband because of who God is and His commands. You respect your husband because of who you are and your character. You respect your husband because you have been given grace and you freely give it. You respect your husband because of your vows at the marriage altar. And you respect your husband because you do indeed love him and desire to please him.

Today's Challenge

This one comes straight from the Bible: respect your husband! Take some time to assess your husband's respect-o-meter. Ask him what sorts of things you do that make him feel disrespected and respected. Listen. Don't argue; just listen.

Application

Write out specific ways you will show respect to your husband today:

_____

_____

_____

_____

DAY 9—KISS HIM LIKE YOU MEAN IT

His mouth is most sweet, and he is altogether desirable.
This is my beloved and this is my friend.

—SONG OF SOLOMON 5:16

Sex is a basic physical and emotional need that men have. God designed our men this way. It's a good thing! Not only do they need sex often, but they need to know that they are desirable (just as we wives need to know this).

A lot of wounds can take place in this area of our marriages if we are not careful. Too much rejection from either spouse can lead to bitterness.

So here are a few action items:

1. *Remember every man is different.* Ask your husband if there are any improvements he'd like to see in this area.
2. *Listen.* If your husband has already expressed some frustration, listen to what he has shared and think about ways you can make a change. Baby steps are fine; just open up your heart to change.
3. *Make sex a priority.* Plan to have it. Don't let life get so busy that you neglect this area in your marriage.
4. *Spice things up a little.* Plan something nice, like putting on

something you feel good in, giving him a back rub, taking a shower together, lighting candles, or turning on music. Take time to make a special moment, and then kiss him like you mean it! You can guarantee he will walk taller.

Paula Rinehart, author of *What's He Really Thinking? How to Be a Relational Genius with the Man in Your Life*, says sex is wordless cheer.[3] It just builds our men up!

Treasure these moments with your husband now, for you will never have these days of your youth back. Enjoy your man and let him know that he is enjoyed. Is there anything greater than knowing someone enjoys you?

Today's Challenge

Kiss him like you mean it. This challenge could be your husband's favorite. I know it's my husband's!

Application

Which night this week will you build your man up with some sweetness and kiss him like you mean it?

_____

_____

_____

_____

DAY 10—ASSESS YOUR MARRIAGE

An excellent wife who can find? She is far more precious than jewels. The heart of her husband trusts in her, and he will have no lack of gain. She does him good, and not harm, all the days of her life.

—PROVERBS 31:10–12

All of our marriages go through different seasons. We all have our ups and downs. We have the newlywed season, then the I'm-so-tired-I-can't-keep-my-eyes-open-because-we-have-a-newborn season, the on-the-go-with-the-kids-and-their-activities season, the challenging-teenagers season, the empty-nest season, and finally, the golden years.

As you look ahead, do not lose your focus on building a strong marriage. Continue to practice these challenges in your marriage:

1. Remember those dating days and what made you fall in love with your husband in the first place.
2. Remember your sacred vows.
3. Remember to ask your husband how you can be praying for him daily.
4. Remember to tell your husband how you admire him.
5. Remember to keep your priorities in line.
6. Remember to take care of your husband and cook his favorite meals.
7. Remember to follow your husband's lead and vision for your family.
8. Remember to respect your husband.
9. Remember to keep kissing him like you mean it!
10. Reflect regularly on your marriage.

Today's Challenge

Pause and reflect on your marriage lately. Has it been a good year for your marriage? Or has it been a hard one? Was it a joyful time with lots of memories? Or was it filled with ups and downs?

Application

Reflect on the last two weeks. How did your husband respond to this challenge? Write your thoughts below:

_____

_____

_____

Remember when I mentioned the book *The Five Love Languages* earlier? Each of our husbands is made differently, and most likely some of what you did spoke volumes of love to him, and other parts were less needful.

Which part of this challenge spoke your husband's love language? If you aren't sure, ask him. If you know, then get busy repeating that challenge over and over and over in your marriage.

If you just read along and haven't actually implemented the challenges, let me encourage you to give one or two of the challenges a whirl. I have received hundreds of e-mails from women around the world telling me that God has used these challenges to transform their marriages.

I encourage you today to stop competing with your husband and begin completing him. Not only will your husband be blessed, but any goodwilled husband will respond favorably to his wife in love and in kindness. Walk with the King!

Part 3

YOUR
PARENTING

One generation shall commend your works to another,
and shall declare your mighty acts.
On the glorious splendor of your majesty,
and on your wondrous works, I will meditate.

—PSALM 145:4–5

With the dawn of the digital age, the timeless truths of God's Word are needed more than ever. Even though I grew up in a strong Christian home, I have found the waters of parenting to be choppy. I am thankful for my mother's wisdom that was woven both into her words and actions in my childhood home. Her wealth of biblical knowledge and scriptural principles that she lived out in our home have given me a framework for my family. Together, let's give our children the best of our time, talent, attention, and efforts.

11

THE INFLUENCE
OF A MOTHER

Talk to men about God and to God about men.

—E. M. BOUNDS, *POWER THROUGH PRAYER*

D o you know just how powerful your influence is? You may think, *Oh, I'm not a mover and a shaker. I don't have much influence in this world.* However, all women have a sphere of influence, whether it's with their husbands, children, friends, coworkers, or within their church. How do you use that influence? Do you use it for selfish motives or for God's glory?

In Acts 13:50, the apostle Paul was spreading the Word of God in every town, but when he arrived in the town of Antioch, the "Jews incited the devout women of high standing and the leading men of the city" to stir up persecution against them. They drove Paul and Barnabas out of town.

It was the *women* the Jews targeted. They recognized our power of influence. The same thing happened in the garden of Eden. The serpent targeted Eve first, and once she disobeyed God, she was able to influence Adam to disobey also. We must follow God closely or our influence will lead others astray. God has blessed us with this awesome gift, and we must use it for Him, especially in our homes.

GENERATIONS OF FAITH

My mom was born into a spiritually mixed marriage. Her grandparents were immigrants from Europe and brought their Protestant faith with them to America. Her mother was Presbyterian and her father Russian Orthodox. Since her father was the head of the home, the decision was made to worship together weekly at the Russian Orthodox Church. Unfortunately, the priest conducted the service in Russian, so my mother and her three younger brothers had no clue what was being said. For that reason, my grandmother asked my grandfather to allow them to stay home from church. My grandfather agreed.

My grandmother sat her four children down in a circle every Sunday and read them Bible stories and sang songs like "Jesus Loves Me." My mom's spiritual training began at the feet of her mother. It was one generation praising God's work to another, declaring His mighty acts.

It is rare to find a family these days that is not pulled a hundred different ways by outside activities. Worldly pressures can smother family devotional times together. It is vital that we as mothers read the Bible to our children. We must not wait for our husbands to initiate a family devotional time. Some husbands will never take this initiative. Be like my grandmother. Step up to the plate. Be an advocate for your children spiritually. Open the Word of God and make memories with your children, and maybe, just maybe, your husband will choose to join you.

MY MOM'S SPIRITUAL AWAKENING

Here is my mom's own journey to spiritual awakening, in her own words:

> At the age of twenty, I married my high school sweetheart, Mike. In 1970, we were blessed with the first of our three beautiful daughters. Having a child makes you reconsider many things in your life. It was at that time that Mike and I became more serious

about our faith. We wanted to grow stronger spiritually so we could be better parents and reproduce our faith in the lives of our children.

We began attending a wonderful church, and I would call our years at this new church the years of our "great spiritual awakening." God placed within my heart a strong hunger and thirst for His Word as never before. Weekly, we attended Sunday morning and evening services, the midweek service, and also a women's Bible study during the day and a couples' study with Mike at night. Our church had a library, and I carted home books, tapes, music—anything I could get my hands on. Anytime a weekend seminar or retreat was offered, we went. God was faithfully feeding me, and I will always be grateful for those who taught and discipled me during those years. I was a big sponge soaking everything in.

A "big sponge soaking everything in"—that's my mom! Her colored pencils were always beside her Bible on our kitchen table, and I could wake at odd hours of the night to find my mom there dissecting the details of Scripture. She kept concordances and commentaries at her fingertips, and this is how she spent her free time. Even now, I sit beside her in the pew every Sunday to worship, and she still furiously takes notes on the sermon in her notebook. At home, she has a huge stack of her notebooks dating back to when I was born. She is still a spiritual sponge, continually seeking God and to know Him more. As a child, I remember that the radio in her bathroom was always running with sermons emitting from the tiny speaker. In fact, just awhile ago, as I dropped my kids off to be watched so I could write this chapter, the radio was still going in her bathroom, with a preacher preaching away and my mom soaking it all in.

Mom is a living example of a woman who is being drenched in living water and, as a direct result, is living well. But she has not kept all this living water to herself. She has allowed God to wring her out and use her to pour into the lives of hundreds of women who have attended her Bible studies over the past thirty-five years.

And ultimately, my sisters and I have been the greatest beneficiaries of experiencing the example of a woman living well, right before our eyes.

WHAT ARE YOUR CHILDREN SOAKING IN?

Little eyes and ears soak in everything happening around them. The influence of a mother comes through the voices she allows to speak into her home. What are your children soaking in from you and from the music, television, or friends you choose to bring into your home?

I find it humorous that from time to time I catch my children watching my teaching videos on YouTube. I am surprised that after all the yapping I do at them during the day, they would want to hear more of me. But they are listening. They are soaking it all in.

Last summer I had the privilege of opening my home to twenty women for Bible study. It was such an exciting night as the women began to arrive. My children loved sneaking in a few snacks before bedtime and peeking around the corner while we prayed. It reminded me of when I was a child in footed pajamas, peeking through the spindles of the stairway and giggling with my sisters while we watched my mom's friends arrive to study the Bible. I soaked it all in, and now I'm squeezing it all back out. One generation proclaiming it to the next.

BREAKING THE GENERATIONAL CYCLE OF SIN

In Exodus 20:5–6, God says, "You shall not bow down to them [idols] or serve them, for I the LORD your God am a jealous God, visiting the iniquity of the fathers on the children to the third and the fourth generation of those who hate me, but showing steadfast love to thousands of those who love me and keep my commandments."

We see in these verses the power of the influence of parents on the generations to come. You see, most likely the sins of our parents will be our sins too. The verse above reads with the word "visiting."

Pause right now and think about your mother and father. What are some of their negative attributes? Before you condemn them for their failings, pause and consider their parents. What are some of your grandparents' negative attributes? Can you identify similar sins in both of their lives? Now think about your own life. What negative attributes of your mother or father are visiting you? God will never punish us for the sins of another, but unfortunately our parents' sins seem to visit us and become our sin.

We see this in the generational line of the godly patriarch Abraham. In Genesis 20, Abraham deceived Abimelech by saying his wife was his sister. In Genesis 26:7, Abraham's son, Isaac, who was a godly man from a godly home, deceived Abimelech also by saying his wife was his sister. Unbelievable, right? But hold on to your hat, because in Genesis 27, Isaac's son—Abraham's grandson—performs the ultimate deception and steals his brother's birthright.

And so we see a cycle of generational sin even within a godly home. Jeremiah 32:18 says, "You repay the guilt of fathers to their children after them."

Our parents' sin may not have originated in our hands, but it has landed in our laps. What are we going to do with it? There is hope found in Exodus 20:6. It says that God shows love *to the thousandth generation* of those who love Him and keep His commands (see the ESV's note for this verse). Sin may visit a few generations, but for the one who takes a stand and breaks the cycle, God's love is poured out *to the thousandth generation*!

"He commanded our fathers to teach [their testimony and the law] to their children, that the next generation might know them, the children yet unborn, and arise and tell them to their children, so that they should set their hope in God and not forget the works of God, but keep his commandments" (Ps. 78:5–7).

Do you need to take a stand and break the cycle for your children and generations to come? My husband comes from a home with generations of divorce. After Keith and I had dated for a year, my parents grew concerned. They wanted to be sure that my future husband understood the role of a Christian husband and the permanence of marriage. So they ordered a Bible study about marriage and met with us once a week for an entire summer and took us through this in-depth Bible study. My parents pulled my boyfriend under their wing, loved him, discipled him, and made a difference in his family line, Lord willing, for generations to come.

THE LEGACY OF LEADERSHIP

I remember going out for Mother's Day to a buffet with all my extended family. As we stood in line, the discussion of how we would do seating began. First one sister spoke up, then another; then I had an opinion, and so did my mother. From there, the husbands chimed in and gave their two cents, and as our family rattled on, trying to resolve the seating issue, I looked at my sister's husband and said, "You are awfully quiet; what do you think?" His answer still makes me laugh: "I think there's a lot of chiefs and not enough Indians here."

Everyone was trying to lead, and no one wanted to be the follower. The reality is, I'm from a family of strong leaders. I could go one by one through each person and make a long list of ways my family members have been leading, from being pastors and deacons to Bible study directors and Bible study leaders, online leaders, youth leaders, urban ministry leaders, Titus 2 Workshop leaders, mentorship leaders, retreat speakers, and more.

When I look at my family, I see a legacy of leadership. My parents effectively raised their three daughters to follow in their footsteps, and God provided three godly men for us to marry and follow in leadership.

PASSING ON THE LEGACY

As the next generation comes behind us, here are ways we can effectively pass on this legacy of leadership:

1. *Recognize that it is the Lord who gives spiritual gifts.* Encourage your children to be who God made them to be. If your children have not been gifted by God to be leaders, then God will have another equally effective place where He will use them.
2. *Persevere in prayer for your children.* I have been praying since my children were born that God would give them spouses who are not just Christians, but growing Christians. If you haven't already been praying for your kids, now is a good time to start!
3. *Equip your children.* Model for them a living and vibrant walk with God so the passion of your love and desire to serve God will be caught, not taught. We must teach them sacrifice, because no God-made leadership comes without first dying to self.
4. *Teach your children about the Lord.* Our children must be brave and courageous to talk to people about God! They must have hearts for others and rich prayer lives to talk to God about people. No amount of biblical preparation and boldness can make up for the lack of prayer. As mothers, we can teach them how to do that.
5. *Help your children learn to be humble leaders.* Elisabeth Elliot wrote of missionaries who arrived on the mission field to discover that they were overqualified for the tasks that were required of them. She went to Ecuador to translate the Bible but ended up washing sheets, working on a broken refrigerator, and clearing an airstrip for the landing of planes.[1] Being a leader does not always mean someone will be doing great, big, huge things for God; most times it requires a willingness to do the tiniest, most unseen task for God's glory.

Servant Leadership

As I look deeper into the legacy of leadership in my family, I see that leadership is really another term for servanthood. I see a family of servants who by God's grace are being used in leadership positions.

Jesus says in John 13:14–17, *"If I then, your Lord and Teacher, have washed your feet, you also ought to wash one another's feet.* For I have given you an example, that you also should do just as I have done to you. Truly, truly, I say to you, *a servant is not greater than his master,* nor is a messenger greater than the one who sent him. If you know these things, blessed are you if you do them."

It is our responsibility as mothers to raise up the next generation of leaders! We must pray over them, equip them, teach them, and model for them servant leadership in our homes. Give them opportunities to lead, pray for others with them, affirm them when they take valiant steps toward leadership, but never forget that those small things they do out of a heart of servanthood is budding leadership. No servant is greater than his Master.

Your influence as a mother is powerful. Don't waste it. Little eyes are watching you. Be the one to stand in the gap for generations to come and break the cycles of sin that have fallen into your lap. Teach your children, as my mother did, to walk with the King!

12

PARENTING IN THE DIGITAL AGE

The impact of your mothering is immeasurable. Raising
your children is life's most difficult assignment, but it is
also life's most rewarding. So I beseech you, give mothering
all of the passion and purpose it deserves and requires
to be done well. Then all the days of your life will be
days ... and decades ... of passion and purpose.

—ELIZABETH GEORGE, *LIFE*
MANAGEMENT FOR BUSY WOMEN

I grew up in a home that some called strict. To me, as the child,
it was a loving, God-honoring, Christian home. My parents
admittedly were strict, but they were amazing listeners and com-
municators. They fully explained why they had made the rules they
had, and they accepted me unconditionally.

So when eighteen-year-old Keith called me for our very first
date and asked, "Do you want to see a movie?" he had no idea that he
would end up at a movie theater, watching Disney's *Aladdin*. It was
the only movie playing that fit my parents' standards. He was from a
home with no rules, so he definitely found this to be a bit odd.

Rewind four years. I was thirteen years old at a slumber party with my cheerleading squad. The girls had just put in a movie, and I was sitting there thinking, *Uh-oh! I'm not allowed to see PG-13 movies . . . What do I do?* So I did the only thing I could do: I faked sleepiness, yawned, rolled out my sleeping bag, and for two hours lay there wide-awake but faking sleep.

Through a loving relationship, my parents were able to transfer their convictions to me. They taught me "garbage in, garbage out"— that we must protect our minds. I am so thankful for this gift they gave me.

Fast-forward with me to the age of twenty. I was a senior in college and with a group of Moody Bible Institute students on a mission trip to Key West. It was our spring break, and we were there to do beach evangelism. The group had decided to go see a movie. I was excited and in!

We arrived at the theater, and to my astonishment, they chose an R-rated movie! There I stood, knowing I'd never seen an R-rated movie in my life and that my parents would not approve. Faking sleep would not work in this circumstance.

I'd been in this situation many times before, but it was when I was with non-Christian friends, so it felt okay to be misunderstood. But there I stood with a bunch of missionary and pastoral majors. Hm . . . now what would my excuse be? I caved to the peer pressure of my Christian friends, and into the movie theater I went.

Two hours later, I left that movie feeling miserable. Why in the world had I watched such wretched behavior on the screen? It was not entertaining at all for me, because I knew the standards my parents had set for me regarding watching movies.

My Parents' Movie Standards

1. *If an unmarried couple came into your home, would you allow them to make love on your couch?* Certainly not!

Well, that's what you are doing when you play a movie in the privacy of your home that has fornication in it. You have invited this couple right into your home to do such things!

2. *If you were taking Jesus in the flesh with you to the theater, would you take Him to see this movie?* Or would you be embarrassed about the sin displayed, for which He was beaten and then nailed on a cross? Jesus died on the cross to save us from the very sins with which we entertain ourselves. Would you take Jesus with you to see this movie? If Jesus can't see it, neither can you!

3. *Your eyes take in images that your mind cannot erase.* Do not play before your eyes images that pollute your mind. Remember, Philippians 4:8 says, "Whatever is true, whatever is honorable, whatever is just, whatever is pure, whatever is lovely, whatever is commendable, if there is any excellence, if there is anything worthy of praise, think about these things."

Do these high standards seem extreme in our culture? Yes, they do, and I took a lot of flak as a teen for this stance in a public school and even in Christian circles. But do not underestimate your children and their convictions. Proverbs 22:6 says, "Train up a child in the way he should go; even when he is old he will not depart from it." These are the same standards we hold to in our home today.

Start talking to your children while they are young about what is best for their eyes to see on television, their ears to hear on the radio, and their minds to take in at the movies. Talk continually about these things. And don't be afraid to be strict, as long as your rules are Bible-based and balanced with a loving relationship. I can testify, as a product of parents who lived out their strong convictions with love, that I am sincerely thankful for my parents' strictness. Will the world change your children, or will your children change the world? The answer to that question is in your parenting.

THE SOCIAL MEDIA REVOLUTION

The media revolution has touched all areas of a woman's life. It has affected our walks with God, our marriages, our parenting, and our homemaking.

We can walk into any gym or field of a child's athletic game and find half the parents staring at their phones—texting, tweeting, Facebooking. I'll admit, I'm guilty too. I take my iPad to some of my kids' practices, and I fit right in with the parents who are distant and distracted. I can't tell you the number of times I've seen a child on the ground, crying, and I've scanned the row of parents, wondering, *Where's his mom?* While the child cries, it feels as if years pass until the distracted parent comes forward to comfort her child. The shells of parents are there, but their minds are far from present.

While it's easy to identify distant and distracted parents, sometimes I have to remind myself that I am guilty of checking my e-mail way too often, being distracted by thoughts about online drama, and making my children wait while I finish reading or writing something online.

My time spent on media *is* affecting my parenting. My children's time spent on media *is* affecting my parenting. Generation X is now raising Generation iY. The landscape for parenting has changed, but we must remember Hebrews 13:8: "Jesus Christ is the same yesterday and today and forever."

My children attended an online homeschool for the first two years of their homeschooling, so they are very computer savvy. It's not uncommon to see my children on an iPad, Wii, or computer. While they don't use these things excessively, this technology is a part of our daily lives, and our children seem innately capable of navigating their way through this maze of technology.

THE WORLD GENERATION iY LIVES IN

- *Cell phones.* Most teens would say a cell phone is vital to their lives. If your teens/tweens don't have a phone yet, then most likely they are begging for one. We can get in touch with our children when we need to, which is a great perk, but a cell phone comes with the danger of access to porn in their pockets. It also invites the risks of children texting rather than communicating with the people right next to them, becoming distant and distracted from real life, sending inappropriate photos of themselves to someone else, and texting while driving . . . just to name a few!
- *Social media.* Social media for kids includes Facebook, blogs, Twitter, and more. It's social; they can connect with their friends and follow healthy spiritual role models online. But if they are in the wrong crowd on social media, it can have a greater influence in a child's thinking than their parents or church. Communication is fast. Our kids text at a rapid pace, using abbreviations and acronyms to communicate with brevity. It is very hard for parents to monitor this 24/7 access to peers, strangers, and celebrity influences.
- *Music.* Generation iY has access to music through many options, including iTunes, Pandora, and YouTube. Music has always been very influential on youth. The music of the youth shapes and molds their thinking, and now it is at a touch of their fingertips! They can download a song with a click. If they are making wise choices, this is a blessing. But if they are prone to having an appetite for the world's pleasures, this can be destructive.
- *Television.* Even after all the online access kids have, television still is a heavy influence. Some homes have

hundreds of cable channels. Many channels are aimed at our children and feed them junk food for the mind.

- *Video games.* A majority of parents would say, "We know that video games are a massive time waster for our children, but isn't it wonderful how it keeps them busy and out of trouble!" I am not against video games, but I do fear it makes children lazy. Also, as children, especially boys, grow older, their appetite for violence and sexual content in their games can grow as their tolerance levels grow.

RESPONDING WISELY TO SOCIAL MEDIA AS PARENTS

So how can we as parents respond wisely to today's media influence on our children?

Be Aware

We must be vigilant and aware of every form of media with which our children interact. If we don't protect them, who will? It is our job as parents to know what our children are doing. Who are their friends online? What music choices are they making? Are they sneaking their cell phones and iPods into their beds late at night? What songs are on their iPods? What channels need to be blocked on the television? Do we have filters on our Internet? What video games are they playing?

Know Your Child

Be aware of your children's tendencies and know your child's weak spot. Is it gossip? Watch the social media and texting. Is it the desire for sexual content? Check their phones for sexting, their online browsing history for porn sites, and their YouTube choices. Is it anger or a thirst for violence? Monitor their video games and music on their iPods. Is it loneliness? Be sure they aren't connecting with strangers (i.e., predators) to fill a void. Screen your children's weak spots and *monitor heavily* their media activities.

Redeem Media

Train your children to use all these things for God's glory. Encourage them to text their brothers and sisters or a new friend from church. Encourage them to put a verse or Christian YouTube video on their Facebook pages. Have them invite non-Christian friends over to play video games to build deeper relationships, and pray for ways to witness to them. Help them start a blog where they share the light of Jesus. Encourage them to follow pastors and well-known Christian writers on Twitter so they can daily be spiritually encouraged by them.

We cannot monitor our children forever . . . and so this is where child training comes into play. We must help our children have godly consciences that are convicted when they go out of bounds with media.

RAISING MEDIA-SAVVY KIDS

All of these media outlets are amoral; they are neither good nor bad. It is the use of them that determines their morality. This is the lesson our children must learn.

As moms, we must train our children to recognize the good use and the harmful use of media. Here's how:

Set Boundaries

When the item comes into the home for the first time, set boundaries right off the bat.

For example, the cell phone will charge in the kitchen each night, where Mom and Dad have access to everything that has happened on the phone during the day. This avoids the phone being used at all hours of the night for secret temptations.

Another example is video games. Consider setting a timer. It's so inconvenient, but how far are we willing to go to keep from raising lazy children? It's worth it.

Regarding iPods, require your kids to get permission before downloading any songs, period. Screen their music, and help them make wise decisions. If there is a certain song they like that you think is unhealthy, talk about it.

Block television channels or hours of the day when they are not to be watching.

Keep all computers in a central location in your home, where sneaking would be difficult, such as the kitchen. My sister has an automatic shutdown on her computer; from midnight until morning it can't be turned on without a password that only she knows.

Prepare to Be Unpopular

If you set the above boundaries, be ready for some battles. It's easiest to have no boundaries at all. But you know better than your children of all the dangers lurking out there. You will have to be strong, consistent, and gentle in your explanations, and prayerful as you guide your children.

Snoop

Okay, I already know that there are a host of moms who really think this is a bad idea. You may think it will ruin your relationship with your children, right? Nope. Let your children know in advance that you will be overseeing their activity on media. (That sounds better than snooping.) It should not be a secret to your children that you are aware of what they are doing. This will keep them from feeling violated. You will not secretly snoop. You will openly oversee their activity because you love them and want to protect and guide them.

STAND YOUR GROUND IN LOVE

My parents set boundaries on music, movies, TV, friendships, books, and magazines during my youth. They were very unpopular for their boundaries. None of my friends' parents had as strict of boundaries as my parents had (both in my public school and in my youth group). I cried at times, complained, fought back, and mouthed off. My parents stood their ground in love. *And I am so glad they did!*

The key is they did this *in love.* My parents talked with me about my choices, showed me in God's Word principles that dictated our choices, and guided me into truth lovingly and gently.

I was able to receive their boundaries because of two important facts:

First, I was loved with an unconditional, gentle, and forgiving love. My parents listened carefully and attentively to my heart, and then, after all their listening, they gently guided my heart. We must have our children's hearts if we are going to lead them into truth. This listening starts the day they are born. Do not be the distracted mom on your computer (I am preaching to myself here). Listen to your children. Listening equals love.

Second, they taught me to fear God. This was key to my obedience of their boundaries. From a young age, my parents taught me how to have a quiet time. I developed my own walk with God. The more I obeyed, the more sensitive I was to detecting things that were unholy in the media. The more able I was to detect unholy things, the more discerning I became. The more discerning I became, the wiser I became, until I came to a point of not needing my parents' guidance. I knew what was appropriate and inappropriate and began discerning for myself. (As my big sisters can attest, I was a real pain as they tried to enjoy the radio. I was known for asserting, "That song is baaaaaaad." This is what little sisters are for, right?)

Proverbs 1:7 says, "The fear of the LORD is the beginning of knowledge; fools despise wisdom and instruction." The child who is loved and has a healthy fear of God will eventually be able to monitor his or her own media. A child who daily is in God's Word and desires to please Him will be sensitive to the junk that media offers and will practice self-control. So we must parent toward this goal: to raise children who love and fear God and who walk with the King!

13

MOTHERHOOD MESS-UPS

*God works through faithful parents who, in spite of
dark and difficult days, walk obediently to Him.*

—Elizabeth George, *A Mom
After God's Own Heart*

Pictures may paint a thousand words, but they don't always tell
the whole story.

I could post picture after picture on Facebook and Twitter of
me smiling with my children, and most would be tempted to believe
that I must have birthed easy children or am some sort of supermom
to be always cheery.

The reality is I have found motherhood to be a very difficult
road. The daily sacrifice and demands of being a mom can be overwhelming at times.

I have struggled with parenting since my firstborn son came out
of the womb! And I have been a reading maniac, trying to figure
out this thing called motherhood! I know that after reading what
I've told you about my amazing mom, you would think that I would
innately know how to raise my children, but it has not been as easy as
I anticipated. I was shocked when my firstborn screamed and cried
for the first few months on end.

Prior to my son being born, I had planned to nurse him for a year. Then something happened to knock my plans off course. Let me take you back to a difficult moment in my life, when I first became a mom.

I held my six-week-old baby in the rocking chair. He was restless and crying, so I cuddled him and began to nurse. He drank for a moment and then cried. What was wrong? Why was he doing this? He latched on again for a couple of minutes and then stopped to cry. We did this for forty-five minutes, and now I was sweating, unsure of myself, and uneasy with how nursing was going. We stopped, and I just rocked him. He was peaceful as I rocked him to sleep.

I went to my computer and Googled "baby crying during nursing." I called my sisters; we discussed it, but I still didn't find any answers. I searched books. Still no answers. Never before had I been unable to will something I wanted into happening. He awoke, we again nuzzled into our chair, and I brought him to my breast. Again he cried and fussed. No one told me that nursing a baby would be so hard.

Soon it was Easter Sunday. I was so proud to bring my new baby out into public for the world to see, but I was worried because our nursing sessions were stressful. I headed up to my old bedroom in my parents' house, where I tried to nurse him, but he refused to eat. Tears welled up in my eyes. *What is wrong with me? What is wrong with him? What do I do?*

The next day I sat with the lactation consultant at the hospital. She weighed him; then I nursed him for forty-five minutes, and she weighed him again. I waited to hear how much milk he had taken in: he took in one ounce. *One ounce in forty-five minutes! What have I done? What is wrong with me? My baby boy is starving!* The lactation consultant immediately gave him formula, and he gulped it down. I went home crying over what I perceived as my first failure as a mother.

It's hard for me to admit I was not able to do what is so natural for so many mothers. I wanted to give my children the best of me. Even though I pumped for months and my son was a very healthy baby, I still feel guilt and shame over not being able to nurse him as I had hoped to do.

I am not saying that not nursing your babies is failing them, but rather, because I was so self-assured that I would nurse my babies until they were one year old, I was disappointed at my inability to reach my goal. God humbled me through this experience. I needed to be humbled, and He is still humbling me daily on my parenting journey.

And so you may ask, what happened when your second baby came along? I exclusively nursed her for five weeks; then my husband went on a business trip and I was alone for a week with the two children. I wasn't sure she was getting enough, and I didn't have anyone to turn to, so I gave up and gave her a bottle. I supplemented with formula because I wanted to make sure she was getting adequate nutrition. Sometimes I still have trouble forgiving myself for giving up so quickly on my original plan to nurse both babies for a year. I felt I'd failed . . . again.

Have you ever lain in bed awake at night and wondered, *Why me? I don't understand these circumstances, God!* Have you ever felt like a failure, as if the rest of the world has it figured out, and you are the only one who just can't seem to pull it together? Your two-year-old won't let you buckle her in the car, your three-year-old bites, your four-year-old hits, your ten-year-old struggles with reading, your teenager is defiant, or your grown child is making poor decisions—and you sit there, helpless.

So what do we do? The Bible tells us, "[Cast] all your anxieties on him, because he cares for you" (1 Peter 5:7).

I remember lying in my bed one night when my children were toddlers and I'd had a terrible day managing them. I lay there crying over my motherhood failures and saying over and over until I fell asleep, "He cares for you, He cares for you, He cares for you, He cares for you, He cares for you, He cares for you, He cares for you." When Satan tempts you to believe otherwise, speak this truth until you find peace. Peace washed over my soul, and on a tear-drenched pillow I found rest. If you are asking God, *Why me?* stop asking and remember His truth: "He cares for you." Rest in this truth today.

When the Expectations Bubble Pops

I remember our first beach vacation with the kids. My son was three, and my daughter was eighteen months. I assumed it would be a great getaway, but it ended up being more work than being home. We stayed in a condo, where I was cooking breakfast and lunch, and our dinners out were stressful managing the kids. Even my husband was struggling with this new dynamic we were facing. Years earlier, we had come to this very spot without our children and enjoyed such a relaxing time together. We envisioned cheerful days on the beach, quiet afternoon naps, sweet moments on our balcony, and delicious dinners out. We never expected how difficult it would be to bring our little ones along.

On the beach, we were not able to sit down to relax. My husband was flying kites and making sand castles with my son while I was chasing my eighteen-month-old daughter as she cheerfully ran around the beach, stuck her head in the sand, and ran into the ocean. I had brought a book to read but never cracked it open. Then a rainy day came, and everyone looked at me to entertain them! I felt like Mary Poppins all day, trying to pull tricks out of my bag to keep the kids busy. I was exhausted at the end of vacation.

I recall standing at the washing machine in the condo, folding clothes and feeling completely filled with disappointment. I told my husband that I wanted one hour alone on the beach. So while he watched the kids, I went down by the ocean and just sat there and cried. I wept and talked to Jesus and told Him how I felt. Releasing those tears in prayer helped my inner wars quiet down.

Looking back, I wish I could talk to that sad girl on the beach and give her hope. I wish I could hug her and assure her, "What you are feeling is normal. You are learning selflessness. You are experiencing growing pains. It's going to be okay, and someday you are going to smile at the memories of this vacation. You are doing the right things. Don't give up, and don't be discouraged. God sees you, He hears you, and He loves you."

But in the moment, I simply hurt; I hurt because my bubble of the perfect vacation had popped, and like a little girl who had lost her balloon, all I wanted to do was sit and cry.

I've revisited those tears many more times through motherhood. Parenting is hands-down the hardest thing I have ever done in my life. It has been the ultimate sanctifier for me. God has used it to humble me and keep me on my knees.

How to Handle Disappointment

The disappointment I faced on our beach vacation taught me life lessons I have carried with me for years. These are the things I learned:

Take Your Disappointment to Jesus

It's okay to cry to Him. He cares—He loves you so. One of my favorite passages to go to when I'm in tears is 1 Peter 5:7: "[Cast] all your anxieties on him, because he cares for you." Dear friend, I have soaked pillows meditating on this verse. Cast your cares on Him. Do you see why? *Because He truly, deeply cares for you!* You are not alone! He hears you and loves you so!

Change Your Expectations

Now that you see that reality does not match up to fairy tales, accept this truth. Turn from critical and negative thoughts, and open your eyes wide to see the blessings that are in your life. Count your blessings one by one. Literally get out a piece of paper and do this! First Thessalonians 5:16–18 says, "Rejoice always, pray without ceasing, give thanks in all circumstances; for this is the will of God in Christ Jesus for you."

Allow Your Struggles to Mature You

James 1:2–4 says, "Count it all joy, my brothers, when you meet trials of various kinds, for you know that the testing of your faith produces steadfastness. And let steadfastness have its full effect, that *you may be perfect and complete*, lacking in nothing."

Have Hope!

Remember, this isn't the end of your story. Step back and look at the big picture. What is God teaching you right now through your trials that will help you in the next season of life? Colossians 3:2 reminds us, "Set your minds on things that are above, not on things that are on earth."

And take heart that you are not alone. You have sisters in Christ who are in the trenches with you. Be strong. "Do not be frightened, and do not be dismayed, for the LORD your God is with you wherever you go" (Josh. 1:9).

THE PRESCHOOL DAYS

As our oldest, Alexander, began to grow and his personality began to emerge, I was baffled. I grew up with all sisters, so this little guy full of energy, zest, and his daddy's smarts really pushed me to my limits. His nickname should have been Flash, because he was always running away from me. I didn't want to be "that mom" who was always yelling in public, "Get back here!" But if you knew me back then, that is exactly the mom I was! I was "that mom" who couldn't get her child to come out of the McDonald's slides to go home. I was "that mom" whose kid would run in the halls at church. I was "that mom" whose child was climbing the store counter in the checkout line. Oh dear! I never expected my little guy to be so fast, nor did I expect him to disobey me like this, especially in public. It seemed that we regularly left playdates with me hanging my head, wondering where I was going wrong.

As I looked at my little guy, I saw a mirror. So many of my son's flaws were my own flaws. It was painful. I would tell him to be patient with his sister while I was impatient with him. I would tell him to use self-control while steam was pouring out my own ears when he got into trouble. But each year as he grew older, I noticed that I also had grown one year older. As he matured, I matured. It was during the preschool years that I realized together we were growing in our walk with the Lord and becoming more like Christ as God revealed our flaws through the flow of family life.

STRIVE FOR PROGRESS, NOT PERFECTION

One of the hardest parts of motherhood for me was trying to figure out what appropriate discipline fit the crime! There are enough books on parenting to fill a football stadium, so reading a book with a formula clearly does not work. I believe in the power of prayer. Each child and each mother is in a unique situation. Don't get me wrong: I love parenting books and have read many, but none of them can replace the prayer of a mother for her child.

Often I found myself saying to my children, "Don't do this; don't do that; stop this; stop that." It was so ineffective, and I learned that I needed to be doing more character training. Rather than always focusing on the bad behavior, I began focusing on the virtues I wanted to see in my children's lives.

For example, my daughter was possessive with her toys in the beginning. Rather than saying, "Don't be selfish," I began focusing on teaching her how to be generous. I gave her opportunities to give and then praised her for it. I remember when she outgrew her My Little Pony collection. Rather than selling them at our garage sale, I stashed them away. Then the next time we were headed to McDonald's on a playdate, I pulled them out and asked her to pick out one for each of the little girls who would be attending. She packed them up and passed them out, and I was able to praise her for sharing. It took very little time for her to learn that it actually felt great to give!

Another example I used when the kids were quite young was a "heart chart." Like most brothers and sisters, my children fought. Since the children were homeschooled, this made for some long, miserable days. So I created a heart chart on our dry-erase board. Each time one of the kids did something loving and kind for his or her sibling, that child could draw a heart on the board. This gave me a chance to acknowledge when they did something selfless, like letting the other go first. Praise is a huge motivator for kids, and this helped me as a mom remember to praise them for their virtues. On bad days we had to erase a few hearts. But when the chart was full, we celebrated with big ice-cream sundaes.

I had to learn to strive for progress, not perfection, and to focus on the character traits that I wanted to see in my children rather than on the negative things they sometimes did.

Not Just Teaching, but Training

Once we hit the elementary school years, some attitudes arrived in our home that were very unwelcomed!

So I thought about what I was doing right. The children were well fed, well clothed, hugged and kissed; their parents had a strong marriage, and we never missed a Sunday of church. They got plenty of toys and candy, and we always had a listening ear. Humph! What was the deal?

There was one specific area in which I felt I was failing: *training*.

My strength as a mom is in the *teaching* area. I am always teaching my children God's truth. We read and memorize God's Word together regularly. When they are in time-out, we go over Scripture verses. They are taught well and know what is expected of them.

My weakness is in the area of training. Teaching and training cannot be used interchangeably.

Teaching is giving my children the information they need to succeed.

Training is giving my children the discipline to carry out what they have been taught.

I identified a few behaviors that were habits in our children's lives. Essentially they were sinful strongholds. My children had become slaves to their habits, and those habits would not be broken through my teaching but through my training and prayer.

Romans 7:18–25 tells us about this struggle with strongholds we all face:

I have the desire to do what is right, but not the ability to carry it out. For I do not do the good I want, but the evil I do not want is what I keep on doing. Now if I do what I do not want, it is no longer I who do it, but sin that dwells within me.

So I find it to be a law that when I want to do right, evil lies close at hand. For I delight in the law of God, in my inner being, but I see in my members another law waging war against the law of my mind and making me captive to the law of sin that dwells in my members. Wretched man that I am! Who will deliver me from this body of death? Thanks be to God through Jesus Christ our Lord! So then, I myself serve the law of God with my mind, but with my flesh I serve the law of sin.

Dealing with Poor Attitudes

Here is how we deal with poor attitudes in our home:

1. When a child rolls her eyes, yells, or scowls, I say, "Please repeat yourself without the eyes rolling [or loud voice or scowl]."
2. If the words he says are inappropriate, I ask him, "Say it again, but this time with respect."
3. When a child slams a door, I ask her to open the door and try again, this time closing it more gently. If it takes us ten times to get that door closed correctly, then that is what we have to do.

Sometimes tempers flare in our home. Let me be honest: disrespect makes me angry. The anger I feel is a red flag notifying me that my children are off course . . . but if I respond to them with anger, I won't be a good example to my children.

My children will only be as disciplined with their emotions as I am with mine.

Training takes time. Lots of time. But Titus 2 calls me to be a manager of my home. I need to step it up and get on my knees in prayer because this battle will not be won in my own strength. I need Jesus' help in my home.

PURSUING PERFECT PARENTHOOD

One thing I've learned is that the mommy struggles I face are common. At one time, I believed I was alone and was afraid to admit these struggles. Then I began blogging about them and realized we are all walking the same road!

I am reminded that as hard as we try as mamas, the outcome is not guaranteed. God was the perfect Father to Adam and Eve. They had the perfect environment, and yet, when tempted, they fell. They chose to rebel. It wasn't God's parenting that was the problem but rather the hearts of His children.

It is not possible for us to perfectly parent our children, and it's dangerous to think we can. The danger lies in thinking that we don't need God to touch our children's hearts to help them obey His Word.

We must remember to be moms who pray and then obey.

My parenting struggles have led me to my knees more times than I could ever count. It is comforting to remember that the God I pray to is the one who turned water into wine. He changes things! And He knows my children's hearts and hang-ups more fully than I do. He handpicked my children for me, and He handpicked your children for you. These are the children He wants us to have, and He uses them to keep us close to Him. He wants to guide us. So, mamas, as you journey along this parenting road, don't forget to be careful to walk with the King!

14

I'M GONNA BLOW MY TOP!

The secret to healthy conflict resolution isn't taking a you-against-me stance, but realizing it's all of us against Satan—he's the real enemy. But this is hard to do when all we see is the flesh-and-blood person standing there who, quite honestly, is planted squarely on the last good nerve we have left.

—Lysa Terkeurst, *Unglued*

I remember the first time I ever "lost it" with my son. He was two, and his baby sister was six months old. I had laid them both down for a nap, and up he popped out of bed, asserting, "Mommy, I'm not tired." I gently laid him back in bed and told him I knew he needed rest. But again, he popped out of bed and refused to sleep. After about five times of returning him to bed, this weary mommy's temper began to rise until I raised my voice in anger at him.

I remember feeling terribly guilty that day. I could not believe the anger that was inside of me. I never thought I'd yell at my children. But there I was—with the situation out of my control, I felt helpless and lost it. I repented and apologized to my son, but little did I know that that was the beginning of a long road of my patience being tried by my children.

Matthew Henry said, "What is spoken wisely should be spoken

calmly, and then it will be calmly considered. But *passion will lessen the force even of reason,* instead of adding any force to it"[1] (emphasis added).

Are you baffled at the fact that your children are not listening to you? Research has shown that when a parent raises his or her voice at a child, a defense mechanism kicks in that helps the child emotionally protect him- or herself by tuning out what you are actually saying. When we as moms go on a long rant about something the child has done wrong, we may feel better because we got our feelings out, but our child has not been brought any closer to wisdom and understanding.

Surprisingly, when we harshly tell our children we do not like something they are doing, all they hear is, "You don't like me." Period. The harshness that accompanies the correction causes the child to take personal offense and not listen.

I know that I'm not alone in this struggle. Mommies everywhere struggle with raising their voices at their children, scowling, speaking in rapid-fire foolish words, or lecturing in anger.

It's interesting to note that the fruit of the Spirit addresses this very issue. The fruit of the Spirit is "love, joy, peace, patience, kindness, goodness, faithfulness, gentleness and self-control" (Gal. 5:22–23). When we walk in the Spirit, we will be gentle mothers. But when we walk in the flesh, we lack all of these attributes.

Which brings me to conclude that we must be in God's Word and on our knees daily, depending on God to help us be the gentle mothers He has called us to be.

THE GENTLENESS CHALLENGE

On my website, WomenLivingWell.org, I decided to run a "Gentleness Challenge." Never in my wildest dreams did I expect the raw emotions and candor that moms would share. As I read through the hundreds of comments that came in, I saw so many moms suffering from guilt, regret, defeat, and even despair.

There is hope. There is hope for all of us. The first step to making a true change is by calling sin, sin. When we lose our tempers and spout off angry words at our children, we are sinning.

The second step is to not remain isolated and stagnant in our struggle. When we are isolated, we become vulnerable to the enemy's attacks. Having accountability with like-minded women, or with a group like a Good Morning Girls group, will strengthen you. You are not alone!

Blogger and author Sally Clarkson has written, "I have always said that a woman alone in her own home with her own limited self, sinful children, and a house that is subject to falling apart, is a target for Satan. Joining hands with other women, having a prayer partner, starting a small group, is a defense against vulnerability."[2]

MY OAK TREE

A huge oak tree stands in our front yard. It tenaciously holds its dead leaves all through the winter. When spring arrives, the new buds begin to appear, and *then* the leaves fall to the ground.

As I look at those dead leaves, I am reminded of all the fruitless words I'm tempted to use under pressure. It's not a pretty sight! It's amazing how running late can make me lose all discernment with my words. Like the oak tree, until I create new life in the space the dead thing holds, I will never change. The oak tree shows us how adding in something new always pushes out the old.

To break the cycle of sin in our lives, we must add in the virtue of gentleness; by default the old vice will be replaced.

For some, this cycle of sin did not start with your generation. Maybe your mom yelled or criticized you regularly, and her mom yelled and criticized her regularly, and now you are repeating that cycle with your children. There may be a stronghold within your family.

We cannot do this on our own. We need the transforming power of God within us to make us new. Second Corinthians 5:17 says, "Therefore, if anyone is in Christ, he is a new creation. The old has passed away; behold, the new has come."

We must control our tempers and intentionally smile more, hug more, slow down, listen, and take a deep breath. When we feel like screaming, whisper instead. Pray, pray, and then pray some more. Take time to write out, meditate, and memorize the fruit of the Spirit in Galatians 5:22–23, as you pursue gentleness.

ANGER MANAGEMENT

Whoever guards his mouth preserves his life;
he who opens wide his lips comes to ruin.

—PROVERBS 13:3

There are several reasons we may feel angry with our children. The book of Proverbs speaks directly to many of our issues. Let's look at a few of the reasons we lose our tempers.

Too-High Expectations

If we hold to the philosophy of "I speak, and the children must obey immediately," we will be angry often. How do I know this? Because by the time my son was three, I had read many parenting books that convinced me my son was to obey "right away, all the way, with a cheerful heart." Indeed, Ephesians 6:1 says that children are to obey their parents, and it is my job to teach them to obey. But the bad news is that they have to be trained to obey, and this takes years and years for children who learn the hard way, and I have two of those types of children!

So my expectations were very high for my preschoolers, and that made my patience very short. James 1:20 says that "the anger of man does not produce the righteousness of God." And I had to learn that my children were ages two and four; they had only been on the planet a short time! It was up to me to get creative—role-play, read life-giving stories, memorize verses with them, model cheerfulness and joy, teach them to try again when they whined, give consequences for wrong behavior, pray with them, laugh with them, bond with them, enjoy them, and praise them. And little by little, after year in and year out of daily pouring into them, I have begun to see the fruit of my labor. Teaching our children to obey is not an overnight process! It's a life-long process, and often God is working as much on us as mommies as He is on our children. In our household, honestly, we have a ways to go. I do not have angelic children. I have normal children.

Exhaustion

The reality is, when we are tired, stressed, and overwhelmed, it's hard to manage our emotions. If you know you had a short night of sleep and your children are on your last nerve, zip your lip and pray your way through the day. Don't require too much of anyone that day; do the bare minimum, and get to sleep as soon as you can. Communicate this to your husband, and ask him if he could help you get the kids to bed so you can go to bed early. Race to your bed! Nothing is going to make that day better but sleep. A well-rested mommy is a blessing to her family.

Disorganization

I am not saying we have to be the queen of order, but I will say that when we are running late, have forgotten an important paper, have lost our keys, the laundry is piled sky-high, toys are everywhere, and the bills are overdue . . . well . . . we are going to be a bit edgy! Waking early enough to get alone with God, pray over our day, get filled with His Word, think through everyone's needs, and prepare for the day before the day comes charging at us will help our irritability levels.

Bitterness in Marriage

Beware if you are struggling in your marriage. There is a temptation to take it out on your children. I have noticed when my husband does something annoying, I may not say anything because it's not worth fighting over. But that annoyance can transfer over to my children. That is wrong. Deal with your marriage issues within your marriage; do not let your emotions simmer under the surface, as the anger will come out when you least expect it.

GO TO THE BOOK OF PROVERBS

Proverbs is stuffed full of wisdom for dealing with anger. Long ago I turned to Proverbs in my Bible, grabbed a highlighter, and marked every single verse that referenced how I am to communicate with others.

Here are some of the verses from Proverbs I not only marked but committed to memory:

- "Whoever is slow to anger has great understanding, but he who has a hasty temper exalts folly" (14:29).
- "A man of wrath stirs up strife, and one given to anger causes much transgression" (29:22).
- "A man of quick temper acts foolishly" (14:17).
- "A soft answer turns away wrath, but a harsh word stirs up anger" (15:1).
- "A fool gives full vent to his spirit, but a wise man quietly holds it back" (29:11).

If anger is a weak spot for you, I recommend you do the same. Mark, memorize, and let God's Word dwell richly in you. There is no greater transforming power on earth than God's Word.

HOW TO GIVE AN EFFECTIVE TIME-OUT

God gave Jonah a divine time-out. He spent three days in the belly of a whale for his disobedience. This time-out was effective: Jonah's heart turned, and he submitted to God. In the same way, I have found that time-outs are a great method for helping children get alone and think about the choices they are making.

So this is how we do a time-out in our home:

1. The length of time correlates with the child's age. If she is three, it's three minutes. If she is four, it's four minutes, and so on. There have been serious infractions that have required thirty minutes on a child's bed or an hour in her room, but these are extremely rare.

2. When they were little, there were times when I had trouble keeping my kids in time-out. I would sit beside them and gently say, "No, no, you have to stay right here. If you get up and leave, we have to start the timer all over, and we don't want to do that, right?" I sat with them and made sure they learned to obey me.

3. Now my children have learned to obey and head to time-out and stay there for the allotted time, so I say, "Think about what you did wrong." Then I go about my own business attempting to keep my cool. I usually pray during this time.

4. When the timer goes off, I go back to the child and ask, "Tell Mommy what you did wrong." When they were younger I would help them and say something like, "Tell Mommy, 'I hit my sister.'" Now that they are older, they know to admit it.

5. Then I ask, "Why does God think that is wrong?" If they aren't sure, I help them along and say, "Tell Mommy because it's not kind, and God wants us to be kind."

6. I ask them, "What do we need to do to make this right?" Then they apologize to the offended person, and we pray together as the child asks God for help and tells Him he or she is sorry.

7. Then we have a big hug-and-kiss session, and that's the end of it.

Let me be honest: this method takes time. I'll admit that it's rarely convenient to add this into the day, but it's vital to the character training of our children. It's important to help the child see that this is not just Mommy saying the behavior is wrong, but God says this is wrong. We want to give our kids a God-consciousness at a very young age. Sometimes while they are sitting in time-out, I'm thumbing through my Bible, trying to find a verse that explains why what they are doing is wrong. Then when we discuss it, I show them the verse in the Bible. The other key to this method is the hug and kiss at the end. I think reconciliation is so important for a child. They need to feel loved no matter what they do, whether good or bad.

Now, I must admit that many times I was tempted to believe my time-outs were ineffective when three hours later there was a repeated offense. But I have learned that perseverance and consistency are required in motherhood. We must not grow weary and give up!

PERFECT WOMEN AREN'T REAL, AND REAL WOMEN AREN'T PERFECT

There are *no* perfect moms, but that should not stop us from pursuing a good and godly life. We are all works in progress. The greatest lesson we can learn is that we are flawed (the cross says that we are all flawed and in need of a Savior), we are weak (2 Corinthians 12:10 says that when we are weak, we are strong), and we must lean hard on God daily to help us be the women He created us to be!

Perfect women aren't real, and real women aren't perfect. We are not left alone in our imperfections. Isaiah 41:10 says:

> Fear not, for I am with you;
> be not dismayed, for I am your God;
> *I will strengthen you, I will help you,*
> I will uphold you with my righteous right hand.

The God of the universe says, "I am with you—I will strengthen you and help you." We need only to turn to Him and allow Him to help us!

Take hope in this: it was flawed mamas who raised the greatest world changers. Abraham Lincoln reportedly said, "All that I am, or hope to be, I owe to my mother." The Statue of Liberty was modeled after the sculptor's mother. Hundreds of people each day go and visit Lady Liberty and look up at the sculptor's greatest influencer: his mom! Do Super Bowl football players look into the camera and say, "Hi, Dad"? No! They say, "Hi, Mom!"

We know of many famous women who have accomplished much in this world; their names are in lights. But think of the many unnamed women who rocked the cradle of great men and women who changed the world. They will forever be unnamed, but their influence is forever with us.

Dear mamas, do not lose heart. Do not grow weary of doing good (Gal. 6:9). We are raising the next generation, and we can't do it alone. We need to daily be on our knees in prayer, not just for our husbands and children, but for ourselves! Walk with the King!

15

SCHOOLS OF THOUGHT, SCHOOLS OF CHOICE

*What if we as Christian moms laid down our education
labels and joined together to pray for our kids, for YOUR
kids, for the kids down the street, and for the kids living
on the wrong side of town . . . what if we rallied around
ALL of our kids and lifted them up each and every day?
What if we went into battle on our knees in prayer each
and every morning for the souls of our children? And not
just our children, but for our friend's children. For the
children in our neighborhoods . . . for ALL children.*

—ANGELA PERRITT, "GOOD MORNING GIRLS"

When I first started blogging, I was quiet about my homeschooling. It was a part of my "About Me" page, and I would
show our back-to-school photos each year, but not much more than
that. But then one sunny day in July, a bunch of our boxes arrived
for our homeschooling year. It was like Christmas in July! I took a
photo of my kids sitting on the boxes, and then, without really thinking it through, posted to my blog photos of the kids with the boxes.
I mentioned the curriculum we would be using. Assuming this blog

post would be like all my others, I was shocked when World War III broke out in the comments section over my choice of curriculum. Women have extremely strong feelings about their school choices that can make navigating this sometimes difficult decision even more difficult.

We have many choices when it comes to schooling—including public schools, private schools, and homeschooling. I believe that schooling decisions are personal decisions. It's between you and God, you and your husband, and you and your children. I also believe that schooling decisions are not permanent decisions. I know of homeschoolers whose kids eventually went to public school, and vice versa, public school kids who ended up homeschooled or in private schools. There is no cookie-cutter approach to schooling, because each parent and child and family is knit together uniquely with a unique set of challenges and skills.

So let me share with you my journey.

My Education Experience

I am a product of public schools. My parents walked alongside me, discipling me and teaching me how to be a light in darkness for twelve years, and when I graduated, I was on fire for Jesus. My parents lived out Deuteronomy 6:6–7: "And these words that I command you today shall be on your heart. You shall teach them diligently to your children, and shall talk of them when you sit in your house, and when you walk by the way, and when you lie down, and when you rise."

Raising a child who walks with the King while attending public schools is possible. I am exhibit A, and my sisters are exhibits B and C. But statistics are not on the side of public school; the numbers of those who walk away from their childhood faith after their teen years is staggeringly high.[1]

I faced spiritual warfare in school, and my parents joined me in the battle. When we moved from our old house years ago, I stumbled across this note from fifth grade that my mom had written to my teacher. It says:

> Due to the subject matter of some of the films shown to the children this week, I would prefer that Courtney not see any more videotapes unless they are rated G. We do not find PG films acceptable viewing for ten- and eleven-year-olds due to the mature themes, profanity, immorality, and violence. We try to monitor all films and television our children see. As responsible parents, we would have liked to have been informed of any films that were planned to be shown so that we would have the opportunity to approve or disapprove. Courtney is willing to sit in the hall and read a book while the other children watch the videotape. Please allow her to do so.

Sure, taking a note like this to school made me squirm, but when I was too young to take a stand with the teacher, my parents stood up for me and prepared me to sit out in the hallway. Five years later, when I was in tenth-grade health class, this would come in handy. I had heard from other students that a movie was being played that would make me uncomfortable. I didn't need a note from my mother. I went up to the teacher myself and asked for permission to sit in the hallway. She said yes. Being different was hard, but I sensed God's presence with me. Mom and Dad couldn't come to school with me and advise me, but God was there! I sensed His presence regularly with me in high school, and it was in these moments that my faith was no longer my parents' but mine.

I learned to take responsibility for my faith in high school. I carried my Bible every day to school because other students and teachers were challenging me. I needed God's Word to help me as I dealt with teens in cults, atheists, and honest seekers of truth. It was a hard time, but it was exciting as I got to have a front-row seat to God at work in the hearts of the lost. Had my parents not equipped me in my younger years so that I knew God's Word well, I would not have been able to defend my faith. Their discipleship was key. Souls were saved, lives were changed, and shining brightly for Jesus became my heart's passion and fulfillment.

However, things didn't go quite as well for my oldest sister. She started high school in the wrong crowd. At some point, my parents took a stand and said, "No more." They told her, "You are no longer allowed to take calls from these friends or go out with these friends after school. We want you to make new friends at school." Oh, this could have gone so wrong for my parents. But their deep love and connection with us helped my sister respect my parents, and she obeyed. She changed her friends, and it changed the course of her life. My parents did the hard things—they protected us, prayed for us, pursued our hearts, and remained connected with us.

My Reasons for Homeschooling

Now fast-forward to me all grown up with babies of my own. I assumed my children would attend public schools as I did (or private schools as my husband attended). But my oldest sister had been homeschooling for about five years, and I was intrigued by her family's lifestyle. My husband and I sat down to have the "schooling talk," and I emerged from the talk, surprisingly, a homeschooling mommy.

Our three reasons for homeschooling were these:

1. We wanted to lay a strong foundation for our children's faith during the foundational years. I wanted to pour God's Word into them.
2. The school district we lived in at the time had some of the lowest academic records of any in the area.
3. At the time my husband was traveling a lot, and I wanted to be able to pack our books and go on the road with him and keep the family together.

Do you see how personal those reasons are? These reasons most likely differ for many of you. This is why I don't believe in a cookie-cutter approach to schooling choices. As you make your choice, bathe it in prayer; God will show you what to do.

The Benefits of Homeschooling

When I first began homeschooling, I thought I knew what all the benefits would be. But as the school years have progressed, I have discovered hidden joys and unexpected benefits. Precious moments and priceless memories are forever held in my heart from these days together. Here is some of what I've discovered.

Homeschooling Is Fun

It is fun to learn alongside your children! The most fulfilling part thus far has been watching both of my children go from learning the sounds of the alphabet, to slow reading, to reading the Bible fluently! What a joy to have taken them on this journey.

We Bring Spiritual Things into Every Subject

As a homeschooling mother, I get to disciple my children while educating them. We can pray and read the Bible anytime during the day. We read the Bible a lot over breakfast and sometimes lunch too. If there's a problem during the school day, we can stop and pray, which is something we couldn't do if they were in school in another location.

No Morning Rush

My children do not wake to alarm clocks and me ushering them quickly to their shoes, book bags, lunch boxes, and coats on a race out the door. Usually as the school bus goes by, we are sitting around our table, eating breakfast and having devotions warm and cozy in our pajamas! I love this lifestyle.

Time to Do Chores

For a lot of kids who are gone all day in school and then involved in after-school activities, giving them chores is a heavy burden. But when the kids are home all day, they have the time to learn how to care for a home. There's a lot of joy found in a family serving together within the home.

No Homework in the Evenings

We get all of our schoolwork done during the day so our evenings are open. Going to a sporting event is a fun opportunity to get out of the house, and we don't have to return to a stressful evening of trying to fit in homework before bedtime.

Sibling Bonding

I enjoy seeing the bond forming as my son and daughter play together and learn together. Of course, they are also like bear cubs wrangling and fighting at times, but they have a connection they would not have if they were separated all day long in classrooms.

We Can Go at Our Own Pace

I have one child who seems to get everything done quickly and is moving ahead in grade levels, and the other child needs me to go a little more slowly and do more review. It's great to be able to go at each child's pace of learning to keep from frustrating them and to give them a personally tailored education.

THE CHALLENGES OF HOMESCHOOLING

While the benefits of homeschooling are plentiful, there are certainly challenges too. I will be the first to admit, when I hear my girlfriends (whose kids are now in school) enjoying some quiet time during the day or going to the gym or to lunch, it stings a little. I've decided during this season of life it is a worthy sacrifice, but that doesn't always mean it's easy or that I don't wrestle with our decision from time to time.

Here are some challenges I've faced during my homeschooling experience so far:

Bad Behavior or Lack of Cooperation

We might imagine homeschooling as a cozy time, but the reality is there are hard moments where the kids do not cooperate or my patience is short. Often their bad tempers cause me to lose my temper. The best way to defuse hard moments is not to react emotionally. When one of my children does not cooperate, I simply pull the child's chair away from the table and tell him, "You sit there, and when you are ready to work, let me know." Now, at first, he (or she) will try to hold out and sit there for a long time, but when the other child is off having fun or having a snack, he will realize it's not in his best interest to sit there forever, not cooperating. When a child and I enter a stalemate during our schooling, I act as though I couldn't care less. I go about my business emptying the dishwasher, rotating laundry, sweeping, dusting, and praying. I go back to the child about every five minutes, asking, "Are you ready to work?" If I get a grumpy look, I say, "Okay" and cheerfully go back to my own work. If we start to work again, and there's a lack of cooperation, then—*zip!*—back the chair goes, and we continue the cycle. Eventually my children get their work done, and I'm able to remain calm and avoid opening huge problems in the discipline area.

Surviving the Stores

The reality is when you homeschool you cannot go anywhere without your children. They are with you 24/7, and it seems stores are the hardest places for my children. I never thought my children would be the ones hanging on the cart, tipping it, spinning in circles, or hopping from square to square, but they are! So I created the traffic-light system. This system first began when I had babysitters. I would put a red, yellow, and green light up on my fridge and a clip on the green light. Then I asked the babysitter to move the clip according to my kids' behavior. If it was green when I got home, they got a treat. If it was yellow, they received nothing; and if it was on red, that meant they had some explaining to do and consequences coming. So when we walk into a store, I remind them they are on green. If they start acting crazy, I tell them, "You are both on yellow." Often they quickly straighten up because they don't want to be on red, and if they behave the rest of the time, I give them grace and move them back to green and they get a little treat by the register.

Surviving the Long Afternoons

In the winter, the afternoons can feel long. So every afternoon around two thirty, we have a quiet time (I call it a sanity break) in the house, where the kids go to their own rooms for an hour to do imaginative play or read. During this time, I can read, clean, nap, or work online. I find that this break is a time we all look forward to, and the kids enjoy it as much as I do.

Cabin Fever

I've had to grow lenient with diving, jumping, and fort making inside my house. I have had to learn to let my kids be kids. Painting, Play-Doh, and crafts are a lot of work to set up and clean up, but the kids need to have outlets for creative play. I try to get the kids outside as much as possible, even in the winter. I bundle them up and send them out so they can run and yell and create and explore. My motto is, "Busy hands and busy minds keep children out of trouble." When kids are busy doing productive things, we all have a better day.

Socialization

The concern about socialization with other children is the number one criticism of homeschoolers. I am not going to debate this issue here, but I will say that my kids are extremely social. Here are some of the social activities they have been involved in: swim class, gymnastics class, karate, flag football, basketball, piano lessons, homeschool class, playdates, family get-togethers, celebrations with cousins, Sunday school, Sunday evening program at church, vacation Bible school, and on and on the list goes!

Overwhelming Workload for Moms

It is a challenge to get all the homeschooling done in the midst of managing a home and a ministry. I have had to humble myself and admit that I need help. As a result, my father has been coming on Fridays for three years now to teach science, math, and history to the kids. It has grown into a great time of bonding for the kids with their grandfather, and I enjoy the chance to have lunch with him weekly and to get some housework done while he schools the kids. If you don't have a family member to ask for help, consider starting a co-op with other homeschool moms in your area or hiring a tutor!

Fear About Being Good Enough

From time to time I've been gripped with fear, wondering if I'm a good enough teacher. My heart's desire is to give my children the best education possible, and I don't want to fail them. On days when I face these fears, I take them to Jesus, admitting my struggles and asking for strength to go forward. He always meets me right where I am.

A DAY IN OUR HOMESCHOOL LIFE

If you were a fly on the wall, this is what you'd typically see on a school day in our home. I wake before the children and have my quiet time, e-mail my Good Morning Girls, and check Facebook and Twitter. Once the children wake, we have breakfast and read from our family Bible that I keep on our kitchen table. We have a special Bible just for the kitchen that I mark off as we read along, in hopes that we'll get through the entire Bible before the children are grown.

Then we do some chores, get dressed, and prepare for school. Usually I give my older child, Alex, work to do on his own while I help my younger child, Alexis, get going. I sit beside her for about thirty minutes. Then we switch, and I work with Alex while Alexis does work on her own or plays for a few minutes quietly with her stuffed animals. Then we switch again or I give them both work that they can do independently, and I stay near them for any help they need.

We go back and forth all day long, pausing for some play outside, a snack, lunch, a shower, or piano practice. I allow no television or video games until all our schoolwork is done for the day, and I encourage a lot of reading in the late afternoons. By this point, I'm tired and need a break. So around two thirty in the afternoon, I require reading and quiet play for about an hour. Then the rest of our evening is typical, with going to sports, playing games, watching television, or playing outside.

There are no formulas or cookie-cutter ways to run a home-school day, just as no two public school or private school experiences will be the same. Seasons come and go, and needs and family sizes will vary. No matter what the choice, we all have busy days—days that try our patience and test our faith. We must prayerfully consider how best to run our homes and schedules based on our own family's needs and yield them to the Spirit's leading.

What Every Mom Must Teach Her Children

Regardless of which school choice we make, our job as parents is to teach our children to "love the Lord your God with all your heart and with all your soul and with all your strength and with all your mind, and your neighbor as yourself" (Luke 10:27). It is not the public school's job or private school's job or Sunday school teacher's job. It is our job as parents to train our children in the way of the Lord. Whichever choice we make, we must be vigilant to teach our children. So prayerfully make your choice as a family, and then walk with the King!

Part 4

YOUR HOMEMAKING

*So, whether you eat or drink, or whatever
you do, do all to the glory of God.*

—1 Corinthians 10:31

As we pull into our driveway, my kids frequently hear me say in a singsong voice, "Home, sweet home." There's simply no place like home. Whether you have a one-bedroom apartment or a large farmhouse, home is where we rest, refuel, and build strong relationships with our loved ones. No two homes are alike. Home is a place where we express our individuality in the kitchen and on the walls. Whether you are a full-time homemaker or work full-time outside the home, we all have in common the desire to make our homes a haven. Together, let's pursue peace, harmony, and organization.

16

JUGGLING HOMEMAKING, MINISTRY, AND WORK

Everything ultimately comes back to the glory of God. It is why we were created; it is why we are saved; it is why we will one day spend eternity with Jesus. Everything is for his glory (Rom. 11:36). Therefore the work we do each day should be with God's glory in mind (Col. 3:17; 3:23). Our work, our sometimes boring responsibilities reflect the glory of God when we do them for him, rather than for ourselves or anyone else. Even here we work by faith.

—JENNIFER THORN, *GOOD MORNING GIRLS*

My husband and I were married in a large church in the country. We had hundreds of guests, and my bridesmaids were radiant in their red dresses and gold sprays of flowers. Our reception was at a restaurant not far from my home. After four years of dating long-distance, my husband and I were finally married and living in the same town together. It was a dream come true! He was finishing his electrical and computer engineering degree at Ohio State University, and I went to work.

I found a job working full-time as a receptionist answering

a sixteen-line phone. Sixteen lines! I was working for a mortgage company that had radio jingles, and when one of those aired, every light on the phone lit up, and I'd break out in a sweat. After ten months, I moved up as an administrative assistant at a brand-new cellular company that had just arrived in town and was starting to build cell towers. This was very exciting! I got my first cell phone. I loved this job. It was right up my alley, very social, and I had a great boss. But in a moment of error, I changed jobs because I had been offered a much higher wage to work for a gentleman I only briefly knew.

It appeared to be an enjoyable job. It was inside a newly built mall, and I worked with mall management. But it was anything but the dream job. I had left a company and coworkers I loved for money and ended up working for a man who was disliked by most of his employees. The end result was a disaster, and I wound up back on the interview circuit once again. I had become a job-hopper—I mean, what exactly does one with a Bible degree do for a living anyhow? At this point my husband was only a few short months from graduation, but I needed a job.

Eventually, I landed a well-paying job as a pager salesperson. For those who are too young to remember, pagers (also called beepers) preceded cell phones. So I went from business to business as the "pager girl" with a trunk full of beepers. In the snow, sleet, and rain, I was out selling pagers. Then the day came for my husband's graduation, and I did a dance of joy!

The School of Hard Knocks

During this season of working my husband through college, I was also trying to be the perfect wife, making homemade meals, keeping up with the laundry, clipping coupons, and cleaning. But I was failing miserably in all of the above departments. Everything I made in a skillet seemed to stick to it, so I burned a lot of grilled cheese sandwiches. Everything I made in the oven was the opposite; it always came out watery and runny. I have no idea what I was doing wrong, but I am still convinced it was the oven's fault!

However, when it came to grocery shopping, I excelled. I clipped my coupons and ran from grocery store to grocery store, finding the deals; but it was exhausting, and I didn't love it as much as I thought I would. As for the laundry, I stayed current, but my husband was very disappointed with my ironing methods. I was surprised that he had an opinion on it at all. It seemed just fine to me. Then there was the cleaning. Oh dear, I did not enjoy scrubbing and shining and only half kept up with it. I'm embarrassed to admit that when we moved out of our apartment three years later, the stain in the bottom of the bathtub was evidence of a shower I had not kept clean.

Why do I share all of this? So you will have hope! If you are a homemaking-challenged woman, take heart. There is hope! I was too. I grew up in a beautifully clean and well-managed home, but it did not rub off on me. Homemaking is hard work, if you actually do it right.

During this time, I led my first women's Bible study and became involved in women's ministry at church. Juggling work, home-making, and ministry was more than I could handle, and I broke out in a crazy rash; it was the same crazy rash I got my freshman year of college when I was overwhelmed. During this time my husband was intense about his college studies and working three part-time jobs. He was aiming to graduate summa cum laude, which meant he had to get a GPA of 3.85 or higher—basically all As. This was a trying time for me, as I was trying to find my way through life and learning about balance, priorities, and choices the hard way.

When my husband finally graduated summa cum laude three years later, we threw a huge party and headed back to our hometown.

QUALITY VERSUS QUANTITY

Since the day Keith met me, he knew that one of my dreams was to be a stay-at-home mom. After college graduation, he finally had the chance to be our sole provider and fulfill that dream for me. The only caveat? I wasn't a mom yet. So when we decided I'd stay home, it was awkward to explain to people that I did not have a job and I was not looking for one. My job was now "full-time homemaker."

The decision for me to stay home, while not yet being a mother, was completely countercultural. If I had gone to work, we could have moved out of our apartment more quickly and purchased a home. I could have stopped clipping coupons, bought designer clothes at full price, gone on fancy vacations, eaten out more often, and had a greater quantity of things. But quantity was not our goal; quality was.

Once I was home full-time, our quality of living changed drastically. First, our sex life blossomed tenfold, and by far this was the most fun season of our marriage. I was able to be well rested, exercise, and learn how to be a homemaker. I enjoyed trying new recipes and learning how to decorate cakes, and I no longer burned the grilled cheese or served watery casseroles! I finally figured it out. I planted a small garden and picked bouquets. I was able to host parties and picnics in our home, do some babysitting for my sisters, disciple junior highers, go on mission trips, serve at church, take meals to families in need, attend my mom's Bible study, and lead my own women's Bible study. I had the sweetest quiet times with Jesus. I was able to pray for an hour at a time and read many books. I developed deep relationships with my neighbors, took Bibles to the workers in the grocery store, and served at church wherever needed. These three years were the glory days.

HOME BY CHOICE

There were very hard moments mixed in with those glory days of staying at home before children. My husband and I were very happy. I thrived. But outside my home I faced criticism for my personal decision to stay home. To some I appeared lazy for not having a job, and others saw me as spoiled. Some felt judged by my choice to stay home, as if my choice meant I thought they should not work. This did not represent my way of thinking at all!

I didn't really have a place where I fit in. No one my age stayed home without having a reason, like caring for a baby or taking college classes. At one point, I started to question our decision. I cried because I was not yet pregnant and longed for children. I was embarrassed when people asked, "So what do you do all day long?" I thought maybe I should get my master's degree, since people respect women who pursue higher degrees. Sometimes the idea of cleaning the toilets and dusting, again, seemed monotonous, and the meaning to my life became foggy. You see, I was perfectly happy with our choice inside the four walls of our home, but when others spoke into our lives with their judgmental comments, I was knocked off-kilter. I knew that our choice to have my husband be the sole provider was not the norm, and I had to get used to people misunderstanding our choices.

BECOMING A STAY-AT-HOME MOM

After three years of working to put my husband through college and three years as a stay-at-home wife, finally I was pregnant! Once again, I faced challenges in the homemaking arena. Shortly before I conceived, we purchased our first home. It was built in 1923. It required some repair and wallpaper removal, and I was very unmotivated. Sadly, it was at this home that I discovered I stink at decorating. I hated removing the wallpaper, I had trouble choosing colors for the nursery, I struggled measuring for the draperies correctly, and the curtain rod in the shower kept falling down because I could not get the spring to work right. I certainly was no Susie Homemaker!

How could this be? I had spent three years honing my homemaking skills, but our apartment had required very little decorating. I felt very inept. But then my baby boy arrived and my focus on homemaking paused as we were enraptured by this new life that had arrived into our lives.

As our family grew, so did my responsibilities as a homemaker. Before long I was back to the days when I broke out with rashes, only this time it came in the form of a terrible daily neckache. Balancing babies, homemaking, and ministry was a beast! I wanted so badly to do it all well, but I learned the hard way that trying to create an immaculate home would forever be a mirage.

I began to embrace our messy, happy lives and find peace in the midst of childhood creativity and controlled chaos. I created systems and rhythms to help me streamline my household responsibilities so I could have more time for the people I loved. I purchased tools and created methods to assist me in my tasks, and I began to experience the joy of teaching my children to work alongside me.

HOW TO CHANGE THE ATMOSPHERE OF YOUR HOME

1. Light a candle.
2. Turn on soft music, or if you need an energy booster, turn on music with a fast beat.
3. Set a timer and go through the house de-cluttering for twenty minutes straight. It's amazing how much we can accomplish in just twenty minutes.
4. Bake some brownies—the aroma is a sure crowd-pleaser.
5. Put flowers in a vase in the kitchen.
6. Choose to smile at your family.
7. Use gentle and encouraging words.
8. Give a back rub, tickle, or a hug.
9. Read a book out loud, or pull out a board game to play as a family.
10. Pray.

HOW DO I CLEAN IN THE MIDST OF THESE KIDS?

An anonymous commenter on my blog once asked, "If I stay busy at home (which seems to be busy cleaning and organizing), what do my kids do? That is a huge area of guilt for me. I am ready to unplug the TV for good. I know I can rise earlier and be more efficient, but I feel as though I ignore my kids a lot of the time to clean the house."

This is an excellent question, and I have found this to be one of the greatest challenges as a mom with little ones. It's obvious that when we compare which is more important—cleaning versus spending time with our children—the children are more important. But I don't look at these two as mutually exclusive. Our goal as moms should not be to entertain our children and corral them from one fun activity to the next. They need to participate in the everyday activities of the home. They need to feel they are a part of what is happening in the home. They should find purpose, comfort, and joy at the side of their mother.

We must depend on God's strength in order to have the patience, endurance, and organization it takes to allow our children to be a part of our daily duties. Let me give you some examples of how I have accomplished these goals in my life. Now remember: I only have two children, which is easier than three or more. But I have learned these techniques from reading books by moms who have more children.

Laundry

My children began helping me with laundry when they were toddlers. They scooted all the dirty laundry baskets to the main room, where we dumped the laundry into one huge pile. Then I would crank up music and allow them to take turns jumping into the pile. (I know; it's gross. But they loved it!) After about five minutes of fun, we stopped and began to sort. My daughter pulled out the reds, my son pulled out the whites, and I did the rest. Once we sorted the items, we pushed the baskets down the hallway, down the stairs, and to the washing machine. Then they each got a high five and a nickel for their hard work.

Truthfully, it would have been much easier to do this myself, but this was a time of bonding and giving them a sense of contribution and purpose. *This took their focus off themselves and onto serving the family.* When Daddy came home, I would brag on the kids' helpfulness and express how grateful I was for them. When they were three and one, they were not very helpful. But now at ages seven and nine, their help is very much appreciated!

Cooking

Another example is cooking. We all know that kids love to get creative in the kitchen, but it is so difficult to have their little hands into everything! So take a deep breath and pray for patience. Remember, you are bonding while teaching them a life skill. To avoid using the television as a way of managing them, I collected as many LEGOs as I could from every friend and garage sale I could find. We had four large baskets of LEGOs that were only allowed to be used in the kitchen when I was cooking. I had a rug that I assigned them to, and they were not allowed to leave it. I would get them started building, and they were extremely creative once they got going. Then, as I cooked, when there was something they could help with, I invited them one at a time to stand on a chair and help. We experienced life together as I made dinner. They helped set the table or taste tested things while building with LEGOs, all while having order in the kitchen.

Cleaning

I continued this philosophy into cleaning the house. The kids used paper towels and a spray bottle of water, and I let them clean anything they wanted to their hearts' delight. Now that they are older, they clean with cleaner and sponges and do an amazing job! I gave them feather dusters to dust as I dusted, and I let them have a turn at the vacuum even when it was too heavy for them. It was great fun for them, and now they are great at vacuuming. Yahoo! My son used to take great delight in wrapping up the vacuum cord, and I praised him for his contribution. Bringing my children alongside me as I cleaned the house was mutually beneficial. We bonded over these chores, and they received praise for their help.

If you have a big task, like cleaning out a closet or filing papers, and a toddler who is going to be way too difficult to have in the room (don't even try it), break this task up into twenty-minute intervals. Work on it each night after the kids are down for bed.

I will admit it is hard work to bring your children alongside you as you do housework. It takes time, sacrifice, organization, and creativity. I don't have guilt after spending this time with the children, but I will admit to complete exhaustion!

Enjoy your children, and watch their eyes light up as you praise them for their great dusting. Admire their strong muscles when they lift the laundry basket! There is no substitute for a mother's praise and delight.

FINDING MEANING WITHIN THE MUNDANE

In Proverbs 31:19, we see the Proverbs 31 woman spinning her own thread: "She puts her hands to the distaff, and her hands hold the spindle."

Let me just say for starters, I cannot imagine spinning thread to use to sew my family's clothing. What a burden! Spinning the thread to sew the shirt that I am going to have to iron—now, that's mundane, hard work. And that's exactly the type of work the Proverbs 31 woman did.

Have you ever felt as though your tasks for the home are mundane, meaningless, never ending, and repetitive? Sometimes we think, *Should I bother to wash that handprint off the window when I know it will reappear tomorrow? Should I really sweep under the table? Dinner's coming, and it will need to be swept again. Do I really need to dust? I can't write my name in it yet!*

Housework can be repetitive. But the Proverbs 31 woman was willing to do the mundane task of sitting down, engaging her hands and mind, and spinning the thread necessary to clothe her family and to make garments to sell and to help the poor.

What is the draw of HGTV, decorating magazines, and homemaking websites? We all dream of creating a perfect home, but in reality, when the house is full of people, messes are being made every second of the day. A woman's work is truly never done.

I would like to believe that the Proverbs 31 woman may not have enjoyed every second of spinning her thread. It was mundane, hard work. In the same way, we may not enjoy every minute of cleaning toilets or folding underwear, but I think we all will admit that we love the feel of clean sheets on the bed, fresh towels in the bathroom, bathed babies in clean pajamas, and a warm meal on the table. The result of our hard work is a blessing to everyone who enters our home.

Now, remember, if you are about to face crusty dishes in the sink and a pile of dirty laundry, do not think for one moment God loves you any less. God does not base your worthiness of His love on the cleanliness of your home. We stand before God justified by the blood of Jesus!

But I want to encourage you, do not grow weary in your mundane tasks. Mundane tasks are the hidden treasure to creating a home that is a haven. Embrace this hidden treasure as the Proverbs 31 woman did, and walk with the King!

17

MAKING YOUR HOME A HAVEN

Why do we love certain houses, and why do they
seem to love us? It is the warmth of our individual
hearts reflected in our surroundings.

—T. H. ROBSJOHN-GIBBINGS,
QUOTED IN *WELCOME HOME*

We all desire to make our homes a haven. After all, no woman wants a cold, messy, or critical home. Whether you homeschool or not, whether you are a mom or not, or whether you are a full-time homemaker or work outside the home, your role in the home is huge! Your husband is the leader, but don't underestimate your influence on the mood and the tone of the home.

Is your calendar full like mine? Do you feel tense, rushed, and even panicked at times when you are running late? Do you feel that the rest of the family is feeling the same way? When I am tense, the rest of the family is tense. When I am crabby, my family is crabby right back at me. I want to have a peaceful home, and I have learned that it starts with me. Proverbs 14:1 says, "The wisest of women builds her house, but folly with her own hands tears it down."

WHAT MAKES A HOME A HAVEN?

What makes a home a haven? Is it having a well-decorated home that looks as if it popped out of *Better Homes and Gardens*? Is it a home that has massive amounts of toys, food to feast on, video games stacked high, and every movie imaginable to view? Is it a certain number of square feet, a separate bedroom for each child, or the neighborhood in which you live?

No. It is not the things we have or the things we do not have that make our homes a haven. It's you, my dear reader; *you* are the key to making the home a haven.

Let's compare two homes and see which one is more like the one you live in.

Home #1: Distant and Distracted

1. *The woman of the home is distant.* She is pulled into her computer, television, books, or text messages, and it's hard for the family to connect with her. She wonders why no one seems to listen to her. The children don't obey her, and her husband is insensitive.

2. *The woman of the home is distracted.* Her calendar is full and her daily demands are so high it's hard for her to focus and live in the moment with her husband and children. She is often late and rushing everyone. She feels guilty about being distracted but is stuck in this rut of feeling overwhelmed and too busy.

3. *The woman of the home is crabby.* She is short on sleep, she hasn't had a minute alone in years, and she really can't see a light at the end of the tunnel to get a break. She feels hopeless.

4. *The woman of the home is discontent.* She doesn't like her home. She doesn't like her husband. She doesn't like one or all of her kids. She doesn't like her church. She doesn't like her neighbors. Truthfully, she doesn't even like herself.

5. *The woman of the home doesn't pray.* She's never lived in a home with a mom who prays. She doesn't know other moms who pray. She wants to try praying but doesn't know where to begin, so she never begins.

Home #2: Engaged and Enjoyable

1. *The woman of the home is engaged with her family.* She is aware of what everyone is doing right in that moment. If a child needs help or correction, she is there to give it. If her husband needs a hug, an encouraging word, or a helping hand, she is right there to care. She is playful and makes time to tickle, dance, or play with her family. This is a woman whose family praises her (Prov. 31:28).

2. *The woman of the home is wise with her time management.* She guards her family from getting so busy that they lose their connection with one another. She dissects her calendar and eliminates things that are unnecessary. She is prepared when it is time to go somewhere to alleviate the stress that comes from last-minute rushing. She and her family enjoy the slow-paced life she has created in her home.

3. *The woman of the home has a pleasant demeanor.* She does not stay up late watching television, reading, surfing the Web, or working. She goes to sleep at a reasonable hour so she can wake cheerfully for her family. She knows that some seasons of life are harder than others, so she is patient with her season of life and is confident that she will reap what she has sown. She works diligently, trusting God with the results of her labor.

4. *The woman of the home is content.* She knows that no home, husband, child, church, or neighborhood is perfect. So she chooses to be content with what God has given her for today.

5. *The woman of the home prays.* She knows that she is weak

but God is strong and that she cannot fulfill the roles of wife, mother, homemaker, and sometimes employee on her own strength. She is completely dependent on God and practices this dependence by daily praying for all of these things.

So I wonder, in which home do you live? Home number 1? Or home number 2?

Let me propose a challenge: Purchase an extra-large candle and light it every day in your home. I start mine in the morning, but you can start yours at dinnertime. Do what makes sense for your family. I often have a candle burning in my kitchen, the main hub of my home. Each time the candle catches my eye, I say a prayer for peace in my home. I encourage you to do the same—watch what God can do!

How to Make Your Home Sing

Edith Schaeffer wrote, "There is a charm in making music together which not only stimulates interest and creativity, but which breaks through whining and fussing and clears the atmosphere."[1]

Playing music is another way to bring peace to your home. I love to play classical and worship music daily, but we also enjoy upbeat music when we are cleaning or letting loose. As I light my candle, pray for peace, and turn on soft music, I am reminded to pursue using peaceful words in my home. I want to maintain peaceful relationships. There is no room for seething anger, tattling, criticism, and back talk when together we pursue making our home a haven.

Need music suggestions? Here are mine:

If You Know How to Play an Instrument, Play It!

In our home, when I sit down to the piano to play, the atmosphere completely changes. All whining and complaining disappear, and dancing and singing begin. This is what the book of Psalms is all about—making a joyful noise unto the Lord. So pull out your dusty instruments and start playing.

Sing

Sing or hum in the kitchen while you cook, in the bathrooms while you clean, or while you drive in the car. Force yourself to open your mouth and let your joy of the Lord be heard by your family. It will be contagious!

Strike Up the Band!

I personally enjoy solo piano music. George Winston and David Nevue are my two favorites. I am listening to Nevue's music at this very moment as I write. My favorite CD by George Winston is titled *December*. I have listened to it for seventeen years. In college, it helped me shut out the dorm noise and focus on studying. It was then that I realized how peaceful solo piano music is. Since then, these CDs remain in the CD player, ready to go at all times, and most times they are playing on repeat day . . . and night . . . in my house. I love waking and walking down my steps to the sound of David Nevue's music. My typical morning includes a cup of coffee, a lit candle, piano music, and time in God's Word. Your musical preferences may vary from mine, but whatever type of music you like, play it while you go about your daily tasks and you'll find a smile on your face.

Play Worship and Christian Music

The sky is the limit when it comes to Christian music, from hymns to Southern gospel to Casting Crowns to the classics like Michael Card. All of this music fills our family's hearts and minds with God's truth.

It doesn't all have to be slow. Music with a beat can lift spirits and add zest to a boring day. Pick a style that fits your mood and family, and get that music going. Once you've determined your music and have it going, it's time to work on ourselves.

USE PEACE-FILLED WORDS

1. *Instead of raising your voice in anger, lower your voice to a whisper.* Proverbs 15:1 says, "A soft answer turns away wrath, but a harsh word stirs up anger."
2. *Don't let someone else's anger make you angry.* Stay in control of your emotions, and do not let the other members of your family dictate your mood.
3. *Remember, yelling at a bud won't make it bloom.* Your home will not blossom into a haven if you are not controlling your temper.
4. *Continue to pray for peace in your home.* Never cease praying. James 5:16 says, "The prayer of a righteous person has great power as it is working."

CLEANING UP CLUTTER

Managing clutter is a huge modern-day problem for homemakers, and it can turn a haven into a hassle. Here are some ways to tackle this problem:

Contain Clutter

Pick an area of your home where clutter collects, and put something there to contain it. For example, I keep a small basket at the bottom of our stairs to collect all the little things that need to go upstairs. Truthfully, I need one the size of a laundry basket because often we are carting up stuffed animals, books, toys, hair ribbons, my purse, shoes, and more. Put bins to catch papers in the kitchen, office, and family room. I also love using buckets to organize under my sinks in the bathroom.

Set a Timer

Set a timer for twenty minutes, grab a trash bag, and walk through your house, throwing stuff away. Throw away old magazines, broken toys, and papers. The rule is, if you haven't used or worn it in a year, either give it away or throw it away. Clutter attracts clutter. If you are a pack rat, this is a challenge. Take this challenge; you won't regret it. And trust me: you won't miss these things! Things will never make you happy. Unused clutter only weighs you down.

Organize Clutter Spots

List a few of the spots in your home that make you visually stressed because of all the clutter. Now organize them with hooks and containers, or move it all to a drawer, closet, or the trash can. Work on cleaning up clutter. Throw things away.

Deal with Spiritual Clutter

Oftentimes we have spiritual clutter that weighs us down. First John 1:9 says, "If we confess our sins, he is faithful and just to forgive us our sins and to cleanse us from all unrighteousness."

Pause for a moment and ask yourself, "What sin have I not confessed that is getting in the way of a peaceful home?" Now confess it. All of us carry the stain of sin. At any moment we may sin again . . . and often we let ourselves off the hook too easily. We justify our sin by saying things like, "I'm just discerning, not judgmental," or "I'm just truthful, not rude," or " I'm just sharing prayer requests, not gossiping."

The earlier in your life you confess sinful strongholds, the better. I encourage you to root out those sins now before they become habits. Do not get cozy with sin. Repent daily. Free yourself of spiritual clutter.

CREATE FAMILY NIGHTS

J. R. Miller says, "The richest heritage that parents can give is a happy childhood, with tender memories of father and mother. This will brighten the coming days when the children have gone out from the sheltering home, and will be a safeguard in times of temptation and a conscious help amid the stern realities of life."[2]

In our home, I'm the family night coordinator. If there's going to be a game night, pizza night, movie night, or a social happening, it's because I planned it. I'm guessing I'm not alone in this. Growing up, my mother did a great job of creating fun family memories. They weren't complex or over-the-top, but they happened! They happened year in and year out, and now the memories of those fun moments give me security, comfort, joy, and a bond with my family that will never be broken.

My children enjoy long evenings of playing Monopoly, watching reruns of *The Brady Bunch*, eating lots of Chex mix, and enjoying lots of cuddles and back rubs, and even wrestling and having Nerf gun wars (my husband loves to flip couches and make forts).

A wise mother knows how to have fun and how to be tender. She knows the healing touch of her hands. Jesus used His hands to touch and heal many. There is power in the gentle expressions of love through warm embraces and cuddles.

Mark 10:16 says that Jesus "took them [the children] in his arms and blessed them, laying his hands on them."

Bless your family with tender, physical love.

THE ART OF COOKING

God created taste buds, the sense of smell, and the eye that is drawn to beautiful things. To please our senses, He created crunchy green peppers, fuzzy peaches, juicy watermelons, sour lemons, and sweet potatoes!

Cooking should not be thought of as drudgery but as an art. Edith Schaeffer says in *The Hidden Art of Homemaking*, "Just as it is good to get one's fingers into the soil and plant seeds, so it is good to get one's fingers and fists into bread dough to knead and punch it. There is something very positive in being involved in the creativity which is so basic to life itself. Home-made bread, home-made cakes and pies, home-made vegetable soup from home-grown vegetables or from vegetable market purchases, home-made jams and jellies, home-made relishes and pickles—these are almost lost arts in many homes."³

I admit the above list does not represent the cooking in my home. Very rarely have I made homemade bread dough; I tend to make quick and easy recipes. But it's the coming around the dinner table that blesses the souls of our families. In Luke 11:3, Jesus says to pray, "Give us each day our daily bread." In America, we are so blessed we rarely have to ask God for our daily bread, but we must remember to give thanks for our food. Bowing our heads as a family in thankfulness to God is a gift we give our children and a memory they carry with them into adulthood.

I remember when I was a child, shortly before dinner would be served, a loud beeping sound would come from the kitchen phone. In the olden days, when a phone was taken off the hook, it would beep very loudly at a fast pace so you were alerted to put it back on the hook. Well, my mom took the phone off the hook on purpose because she did not want our time around the table to be interrupted. She guarded our family dinnertime.

Mom always had a home-cooked dinner and dessert on the table. We opened in prayer and then ate and talked up a storm. As my sisters and I got into our teen years, we had activities that would get in the way of family dinner; but when we arrived late in the evening, there was always a home-cooked meal and my mom in the kitchen, ready to feed us and talk with us about our day. I strongly believe this is one of the reasons that all five of us as adults are close to one another and to our heavenly Father.

Growing up, this seemed normal; I assumed all families had dinner together regularly. Then I married my husband. He did not grow up in a home like this. Some of his favorite memories from childhood are from the holidays when his mom cooked a big meal and they ate around the dinner table; this is when I realized how special our nightly ritual was.

Recently I told my children, "A lot of families eat with the television on rather than talking." They were surprised, and they felt as though they were missing out. They wanted to eat with the television on too!

Children and teens who eat a family dinner tend to get better grades, are less likely to do drugs, have healthier eating habits, and communicate better with their parents . . . and yet baseball coaches schedule practice *right* in the middle of dinnertime. What do we as moms do? We have to get creative! We need to move dinner to a later time or we have to say no to obligations that stand between us and our family time. We must not cave in and abandon the tried-and-true practice of eating dinner together. It truly is important.

Edith Schaeffer says, "Food cannot take care of the spiritual, psychological and emotional problems, but the feeling of being loved and cared for, the actual comfort of the beauty and flavour of food, the increase of blood sugar and physical well-being, help one to go on during the next hours better equipped to meet the problems."[4]

Alexis and I connect over peeling potatoes and cracking eggs. She loves to stir a pot of soup or pour the ingredients into the mixing bowl. She enjoys making meals appealing by pulling out fancy napkins and china alongside me. We don't have to have guests to pull these things out; we make our home a haven when we treat our own family as worthy of these special touches.

Let's bless our families this week with special surprises from our kitchen! And while the candles are lit and the music is going, take your husband by the hand and slow dance cheek to cheek—the children will love it! Grab them by the hands, too, and swirl them around. Have fun together as a family as you walk with the King!

18

ROUTINES THAT BRING REST

Home ... To me it says so much about being cozy in my own nest, about being where I belong, about tending to the most important parts of my life. Being at home means savoring that sense of safety and retreat, even when I'm hard at work. The world may be whizzing by outside, but here I am safe, tranquil, peaceful, productive. At home.

—EMILIE BARNES, *WELCOME HOME*

I went to the attic the other day. I needed something that was up there. Boy, was it hot! Then I walked to the back of the attic and stood there. Hm. I could not remember why I had gone up there. What exactly was it that I needed? I wandered around a little to see if I would remember, and nothing came to me. So I stood there and thought, *I'm losing my mind!*

I began to break out in a sweat. It was hot up there, but I would not budge because I knew there was something I needed. Just what was it? I thought through what I was doing right before I went up to the attic. Nothing rang a bell. Argh!

I wracked my brain, when it finally hit me—a bottle of lotion! Yes, I buy my lotion in bulk when my favorite store has big sales, and I store it in the attic. So I got my lotion and headed back downstairs, all sweaty!

Do you ever feel you have so much going on that you are losing your mind?

How often do we take the time to watch the sun rise and meet with Jesus peacefully in the morning? Have we taken the time to meditate on God's Word and let the Psalms comfort us, the Proverbs counsel us, the Gospels draw us nearer to Jesus, and Revelation fill our hearts with hope?

Have we sat with God and just talked with Him about our struggles, pains, and frustrations, giving Him all our cares in exchange for peace? Are we seeking God's will for our lives or some answers to some difficult situations? Have we sat still long enough to renew our minds in His Word so we can know His will rather than lose our minds?

Because we do not rest, we miss hearing God's voice. Psalm 23 comes to mind: "The LORD is my shepherd; I shall not want. He makes me lie down in green pastures. He leads me beside still waters. He restores my soul. He leads me in paths of righteousness for his name's sake."

Are you experiencing the green pastures, the quiet waters, and the restoration of your soul that Psalm 23 speaks of, from resting with your Shepherd?

Remember how the crowds pressed in on Jesus everywhere He went? Everywhere He turned, there was a need unmet, and though there was so much to do . . . He withdrew to rest. Luke 5:16 says, "But he would withdraw to desolate places and pray." If Jesus needed alone time with God, then certainly we do. Just think of the wisdom He wants to impart to you, the strength and the peace you may be missing out on.

Give yourself permission not to have your to-do list all checked off in order for you to rest and get alone with God.

Schedules That Streamline

I love a good weekly schedule. By nature a schedule sounds rigid, but in reality it is very flexible. It simply streamlines my week. Every fall I create a new set of schedules for my homeschool day, cleaning, and meals. Have I ever stayed on schedule perfectly? Nope. Never. But it's a great guide, and it helps me sort out my priorities and bring order to my mind. I need this or chaos quickly erupts.

Routines streamline some of the things I really don't enjoy doing. For example, my cleaning schedule—I love the alliteration, which makes it easy to remember:

Mondays—Menu and Market (grocery shop)
Tuesdays—Toilets, Tubs, and Towels (bathrooms)
Wednesdays—Wash (laundry)
Thursdays—Dust
Fridays—Floors

Will following this schedule make my house all clean at once or ready for a dinner party? No. But most weeks it is sufficient in making sure I complete the basics without getting overwhelmed. The more I practice the schedule, the less it is a schedule ruled by the clock and the more it simply becomes a routine or rhythm in our household.

I do our menu the same way:

Mexican Mondays
Tomato-y (Italian) Tuesdays
What the Children Like Wednesdays
The Breakfast Dinner Thursdays
Fishy Fridays
Slow-Cooker Saturdays
Simple Soup or Sandwich Sundays (often we go to Subway)

Everything in nature has a rhythm; seasons flow from summer to fall to winter to spring and then back to summer again. The sun rises and sets and the tides come in and out on a rhythm. But even in nature there are storms, tornadoes, and hurricanes—unexpected events that interrupt the routines. I know my family will face storms and moments when the unexpected happens and our schedules will have to flex.

For some, organization does not come naturally; I fall into that category! Now, you may think that I naturally love schedules, but the truth is I struggle in this area. I have read many good books, systems, and websites to come to this place in life (as my mom and husband can testify, I am apt to overbook myself). My schedule is my secret weapon that makes me appear to be able to do a lot with ease, when really it's just a little bit of discipline and a lot of turning a blind eye when I don't get it all done.

If you regularly feel overwhelmed by all you have to accomplish in a day, week, and month, then I suggest you give yourself a few hours with your calendar. Sit down and list all that you have to accomplish each day. For example, consider the fact that the average woman will plan, shop for, cook, and clean up more than a thousand meals just this year! Wouldn't it benefit us all to find a system that works, is efficient, and stays within our budget? This is important. This is our time, something we don't want to waste.

Write out your priorities. Decide when you can accomplish these things. Pick a time, and work toward your goals.

It may seem like a lot of work to put a routine into place, but in the end you will save a lot of time—and guess what you get to do with your free time? Relax and cuddle with your chicks and nuzzle with your hubby. Enjoy the fruit of your labor! Proverbs 31:28–29 says, "Her children rise up and call her blessed; her husband also, and he praises her: 'Many women have done excellently, but you surpass them all.'"

THE IDEAL OF THE 1950S HOUSEWIFE

My grandmother, a mother of four, was a 1950s wife. She is also a Proverbs 31 woman. Were all wives in the 1950s also Proverbs 31 women? No. The two terms are not equal. I know nostalgia makes us believe the old days were better, but what distinguishes a 1950s wife from a Proverbs 31 one? Her fear of God (Prov. 31:30).

Grandma's life was full and busy as she lovingly cared for her family. She served God by serving her family. She worked with willing hands (v. 13), she set about her work with strength (v. 17), she looked well to the ways of her household, and she did not eat the bread of idleness (v. 27). And the most beautiful part was she feared the Lord (v. 30).

My grandma had a weekly schedule that she jotted down in a journal. My mother rattled it off as quickly as my grandmother! One strong similarity of the 1950s wife and the Proverbs 31 wife are their household duties.

A 1950S HOMEMAKER'S SCHEDULE

Here's my grandmother's schedule and what a woman's work looked like in the 1950s:

- *Mondays—Wash Clothes.* She washed the clothes by hand in sudsy water; then she'd wring them, rinse them, wring them, and hang them outside to dry. This took all day.
- *Tuesdays—Iron.* She ironed everything—shirts, pants, and underwear. There was no such thing as permanent press fabrics; everything was very wrinkly. This took all day.
- *Wednesdays—Mend and work on new sewing projects.* She sewed patches onto pants and mended socks. My

grandmother sewed all of my mother's clothes until she reached the middle of high school.

- *Thursdays—Clean the bedrooms and bathrooms.*
- *Fridays—Clean the living room, dining room, and kitchen.* Grandma baked every day. She made cinnamon rolls, pies, doughnuts, and cakes from scratch.
- *Saturdays—Prepare for Sunday by cooking double meals and giving baths.* Grandma always made hamburgers for dinner on Saturdays because they were fast. Then she focused on the Sunday roast and sheet cake that they would eat after church.
- *Sundays—Worship and day of rest.*

My grandparents only had one car, which was normal in those days. Grandpa did the grocery shopping, and Grandma planted a garden. She grew corn, tomatoes, green beans, lettuce, potatoes, carrots, pears, peaches, cherries, and grapes. Then she canned it all for the winter.

Do I want to be a 1950s wife? No. I certainly love my modern-day conveniences! But if there's a 1950s wife I'd like to emulate, it's not June Cleaver but my grandmother. Her God and her family were of prime importance, and her daily priorities show this to be true.

As Proverbs 31:31 says, "Give her of the fruit of her hands, and let her works praise her in the gates."

My grandmother's works are worthy of my praise. I pray that our generation would be remarkable in our care for our families and homes and that our works, too, would be worthy of praise.

SUNDAYS IN THE 1950S

Life was different in the 1950s. Many states enforced a "blue law" that required stores and most places of work and business to be closed on Sundays. This made it possible for most people to be in church. My father recalls that almost everyone went to church. This social expectation even crossed into the classroom. My father recalls his public school fifth-grade teacher asking on Monday mornings who went to church, and they had to raise their hands. His family sometimes missed, and he was embarrassed he couldn't raise his hand. Could you imagine that now in our schools?

My grandmother usually spent her Saturdays preparing for her Sunday day of rest. As I mentioned earlier, this meant she cooked her Saturday meal (usually simple hamburgers) plus her Sunday meal (usually a roast and sheet cake). After attending church on Sundays, she merely reheated the prepared food and served it.

Following the meal, they spent time with friends and relatives. They would talk and visit all afternoon and then return back to Sunday evening church. My father's family would often go on a Sunday drive to look at the countryside or skip rocks in a lake.

Sunday dress was very different. Men would not even consider going to church without a suit jacket and tie. Even the little boys wore suit coats. And on ninety-degree days, in churches with no air-conditioning, the men just sat there sweating. The women also wore their best dresses and shoes and hats.

What can we learn from Sundays in the 1950s?

Make Worship a Top Priority

It has become culturally acceptable to not attend church on Sundays (and trust me: no teachers are asking!) or to miss for less-than-urgent reasons. Sports, parks, boating, or doing yard work is generally an acceptable way in our culture to spend our Sunday mornings.

While we do not have a legalistic God, and this list is rather legalistic, I just want to point out that God's Word says these things must not be a "habit." Hebrews 10:25 says we should "not [be] neglecting to meet together, *as is the habit of some*, but [should be] encouraging one another, and all the more as you see the Day drawing near." I do not want to impose needless guilt on anyone, so the question you need to ask yourself is: "Is this a onetime thing or a habit?" Only you can answer that question for yourself.

Prepare for the Day of Worship

Your temperament on Sundays affects your family and their ability to enjoy the day. If your mornings are *crazy*, and everyone is on edge because you have not prepared on Saturdays nor gotten up early enough on Sundays, determine to set time aside on Saturdays to have all your ducks in a row. Proverbs 31:27 says a wise woman "looks well to the ways of her household and does not eat the bread of idleness." Do not let your idleness on Saturday night affect the Lord's Day of worship. Be diligent.

Make Sundays a Family Affair

Our culture is very active and busy. Families become disjointed as each individual does his or her own thing. Families are breaking down as a result. Sundays are a great day to slow down and reconnect. Be purposeful in thinking through how you can create a simple day for the family to be together.

Dress Your Best

Now again, here's where I do not want to cross the line into legalism. I know in many churches jeans are acceptable and God truly is judging our hearts, not our outerwear, *but* that being said, put some thought and time into what your family wears on Sundays. If you were going to meet the president today, what would you wear? Be sure you don't respect the president more than God.

More importantly, modesty is a huge issue in church today. In the '50s, women were modest in church. If you are a mommy of little ones, be sure your dresses are not too low or too short. Too often men get an eyeful when moms are leaning down to pick up babies. I know it can be completely unintentional. Just guard your body and modesty. Double-check your dresses by leaning over in the mirror. If cleavage shows, put a tank on under your dress.

I don't want to return to the 1950s, but I do think there are a few things we can learn from the Titus 2 women of the '50s. They worked hard during the week, but they also knew how to stop and rest. Think through the above list and try to implement one of these things this Sunday!

YOU NEED A BUBBLE BATH!

"Go take a bubble bath."

"You should go to bed early tonight and get some extra rest."

"Let me get you a warm cup of coffee and a book, and you sit down and take a break."

No one ever says these things to you, do they? And so, I'm guessing you rarely treat yourself to any of these. You rarely allow yourself to relax. I know this because you are just like me. I mistakenly believe I can go and go and go without consequence.

A bubble bath is something *completely* free that only you can give yourself. It is something we do alone in a place where we can stop the rush, hush, reflect, and see clearly. I know there is a temptation at the end of a weary day to turn on the television and have a snack. This is a common stress reliever, but it doesn't get us alone with God and it doesn't give us the peace our souls long for. Television is empty. God's Word is full.

BUBBLE BATH BASICS

An awesome bubble bath takes planning, so here's what you need:

1. Privacy—all children asleep and husband aware that you don't want to be interrupted
2. Hot water and loads of bubbles—preferably ones that smell yummy!
3. Some soft classical music
4. A hand towel rolled up as a pillow

---

5. A cold drink to set beside the tub
6. Your Bible, a good Christian book, or simply quietness—reflecting on your day and talking with God in prayer

Optional: a lit candle

Now sit back, *relax*, and be alone with just you and God. Twenty minutes, and *voilà*! You emerge a new woman.

Do not wait until the house is clean and the laundry is all folded. It will never be all done! Give yourself permission in the midst of your busyness to have a few moments of peace.

WEARY HOMEMAKER

I remember feeling a tinge of guilt after the *Rachael Ray* episode aired. There are so many wives and moms who are just like me. I am an ordinary wife doing ordinary work, but I serve an extraordinary God! You deserve to be in the spotlight too. I wish I could have packed you all in my bags and said, "Look, I am not alone; there are many women out there who are just like me!"

Being a devoted homemaker is hard work. The daily grind of endless dirty dishes, training issues, messes, and laundry are exhausting. God sees you. He knows your babies are sick today, your dryer broke, or your husband just lost his job. Do not be discouraged and downcast by the daily difficulties you face. Your work is significant!

If you feel empty and as though you need strength so you have more to give to your family, sit down with your Bible. Have a huge dose of daily bread and living water, and then go forward with peace and serve your family, not with your own strength, but with God's. And in heaven one day, your reward awaits you—and trust me: it will be much better than ten minutes on the *Rachael Ray Show*! As you fulfill your high calling as wives, moms, and homemakers, continue to walk with the King.

19

MEDIA AND YOUR HOMEMAKING—TIMES HAVE CHANGED!

The Bible opens with God working. The proportion
was six days of work to one day of rest, a formula
that has never been improved upon.

—ELIZABETH ELLIOT, *THE SHAPING*
OF A CHRISTIAN FAMILY

Do you remember when women used to have to butcher and pluck their own chickens? Me neither!

All my life chicken has come in a plastic-wrapped package, ready for seasoning and the oven. Or even better, I can buy rotisserie chickens cooked and ready to serve. It's wonderful! But our great-grandmothers did it a bit differently.

My grandmother explained to me that a chicken in a box used to be delivered by a local farmer to her mother. Her mother would put the chicken between her legs (and if you are squeamish, skip the rest of this paragraph) and twist its head off. Then she would drain the blood. After draining the blood, she fired up a pot of boiling water and soaked the chicken until the feathers could easily be plucked. She would place the chicken into the sink, pluck it, and take all the inside stuff out. Then after all of the above, she could begin the process where we begin our process today—seasoning it and cooking it.

Seriously? I'm not sure we should ever complain about having to cook for our families. We are so blessed to live in a day when we can quickly make tasty meals for our families and not have to deal with feathers!

Then there was the laundry. I find it a challenge to get all my laundry washed, dried, folded, and into the drawers in a timely manner. But as I mentioned in chapter 18, not too long ago, women washed their clothes by hand in sudsy water, put them through a wringer, rinsed the clothes by hand, put them through another wringer, and then hung them outside or in the basement to dry. Then (this is the *kicker* to me) every single item had to be ironed! Ugh! Did I mention I hate ironing and avoid buying clothes that need to be ironed? There was no such thing as permanent press, so everything, including underwear, was wrinkly and in need of being ironed. It would be one long day if I ironed every item I wash!

Now, I must admit, ironing can be fun when I'm watching my favorite television show, but the ladies of old did not have televisions to entertain them while they ironed. Which brings me back to my first point: we have to try to not complain. We are blessed homemakers!

Since our great-grandmothers sewed much of their clothes, sewing and mending was a large part of a woman's day. My grandmother says how excited she was when iron-on patches were invented! Oh boy, don't get me started. I am so thankful for stores like Target, where I can get matching sets of clothes for five bucks a pop!

The time our generation has been given by convenience stores and products is a gift! But we have managed to fill up the extra time with all sorts of things. I feel it. There are days where I look around and can't figure out where the day has gone and why the house looks like a tornado hit.

Where is all the free time that convenience stores and products have given us? Can I suggest where one large portion of that time has gone? Media!

I am not saying this is the only time zapper we are experiencing, but it's a large one, so let me be transparent for a moment.

1. I am guilty of being on my computer while laundry piles up.
2. I am guilty of letting my children out of chores so I can have more time answering e-mail in the morning rather than overseeing them with their chores. As a result, the upstairs is messy for the day. But the kids love it!
3. I am guilty of staying up too late following a Twitter stream rather than doing something more productive around the house, like cleaning out a closet or baking a batch of cookies for the family.
4. I am guilty of admiring someone else's decorating or garden online rather than decorating my own home or tending to my own garden . . . I have completely botched gardening because we did not weed often enough.
5. My homeschool room went undecorated for a year while I admired all the amazing homeschool rooms online! It's so ironic. Media gives me a plethora of ideas, but in the rush of life, I was not slowing down to implement them.

How Social Media Can Help Homemakers

I have read many stories written by women who struggle desperately with the skills of homemaking. Most of these women grew up in homes with either a mother who did not do much homemaking or an absent mother. They feel frustrated as they try to manage their homes without any previous training or an example to follow.

The online world has created a community where women can

talk shop. We share recipes, decorating tips, how-to tutorials, and all sorts of creative ideas. I love the synergy and creative juices that flow as women who are like-minded connect and create and dream and make their ideas a reality. It is simply fascinating to see God's character displayed in the women sharing their gifts and talents.

The key to using social media wisely is to implement the ideas in your home! It's really that simple. If we spend hours browsing online, it in no way benefits our family. But if we print the idea and do it, we have just blessed our family!

I used to spend time browsing magazines. I would pull out decorating ideas or clip recipes. I no longer do this. Now I hop on the Web, Google what I'm looking for, and a million women are there with blog posts on how to do the very thing I need. If there is something we want to learn, there is no excuse; we can learn it. It is all available online—from knitting, to sewing, to baking and sautéing, to decorating and organizing. Some of these ladies are geniuses!

The danger comes when the ugly green-eyed monster appears. Jealousy rears its ugly head or we feel guilty about the fact we are not as good at a certain skill as another. Discontentment with our homes can grow and take over. We can falsely believe that other women have ten talents while we were only given one, and miss the fact that usually the women we see are very good in their one trade but struggle in other areas. The more we feed negative thoughts and self-talk, the worse it can become, until we are discouraged and feel worthless because of the comparison games.

Be You

You should never seek to be someone else; you are amazing. God created you with all those gifts and talents so different from others that your life would be wasted if you tried to be like someone else.

As blogger Chris Brogan says, "Be you hard. You're going to do so much more than me. You're going to change your space. You're going to . . . nail it. Why try to be me. I'm going to falter at some point and you'll have forgotten about comparisons. You should. Be you. It's way more fun."[1]

The biblical principles in this book should be the same for all of us, but how we apply them will look different in every home. We must be careful that we are not followers of everyone online but rather followers of Christ.

Jesus Christ said in Luke 9:23, "If anyone would come after me, let him deny himself and take up his cross daily and follow me." I am learning how to live the crucified life one step, one day, one month, one season, one year, one decade at a time. God has used marriage, parenting, and homemaking to show me my ugly sin and to sanctify me. That is the process we all face: sanctification, or becoming more like Christ. On my own, I am feeble at best.

Rejoice in your uniqueness. Have fun being you! Delight in your individuality.

PURSUING THE PROVERBS 31 WOMAN

Don't worry about what others are doing or their style of homemaking; pursue the Proverbs 31 woman. The Proverbs 31 woman "looks well to the ways of her household and does not eat the bread of idleness" (v. 27). Let's pursue making our homes havens for our families by being organized, consistent, and self-disciplined. Let's aim to not be distracted and distant, but always there for our loved ones with a hug, a smile, a warm meal, clean sheets, and some lines in the rugs from our vacuum. It is one way we can show, without words, our love to our families. This is how our Christian great-grandmothers did it as they walked with the King.

20

DISCIPLINE AND DILIGENCE: THE PROVERBS 31 WOMAN

*Ordinary work, which is what most of us do most of
the time, is ordained by God every bit as much as is the
extraordinary. All work done for God is spiritual work
and therefore not merely a duty but a holy privilege.*

—ELIZABETH ELLIOT, *THE SHAPING
OF A CHRISTIAN FAMILY*

Have you ever wondered who the nameless, perfect woman that Solomon wrote about in Proverbs 31 was? Was she for real? The answer is no and yes. Let me explain.

There once was a prince who would one day be a king. While he was young, his mother wisely trained her son on how to find a virtuous wife. She went through the alphabet one letter at a time, giving him attributes that he was to seek out in his future wife. Using the alphabet in this manner made it easier for her son to remember and perhaps even memorize what he was looking for in his ideal wife. Thus, we have the writings of Proverbs 31.

So was the Proverbs 31 woman real? Did she have a name? No. Proverbs 31:1 says, "The words of King Lemuel. An oracle that his mother taught him . . ." Then verses 2–9 are instructions on how to be a godly king. She taught him to be on guard against promiscuity and drunkenness and encouraged him to tend to the poor. Then in verses 10–31 she instructed him on how to find a godly wife. The Proverbs 31 woman has no name, just a superior character.

But we must ask: Would King Lemuel's mother give him detailed instructions on what to look for in a wife if there were no women who could possibly have this kind of character? In verse 10, we see that she is a rare treasure, but she does exist.

The key to remember is that this passage of Scripture is not what this woman completed in a day but rather what she completed in a lifetime. Don't let this proverb overwhelm you; rather, let it give you hope. Give yourself time to grow and mature as you strive to be like her.

How to Be a Treasure to Your Husband

An excellent wife who can find? She is
far more precious than jewels.

—Proverbs 31:10

A noble wife is rare and extraordinary, just like jewels! Do you want to be a treasure to your husband like a rare gem? Then you need to learn to possess a noble character.

Here is what a wife of noble character does *not* look like:

1. She does not compete with her husband.
2. She does not mope around and complain about her housework.
3. She does not overspend and put her family into debt.
4. She is not bored, discontent, greedy, or selfish.

5. She does not gossip and slander others.
6. She does not spend her days doing leisurely shopping, texting, e-mailing, Web browsing, watching late-night movies, and sleeping in.
7. She does not criticize, mock, or disrespect her husband.
8. She does not embarrass her husband or children.
9. She does not let her outer beauty take precedence over her inner beauty.
10. She does not take God's Word lightly.

A wife of noble character, who can find? She is rare! And when she is found, her value is priceless. She is a treasure to her husband. I want to be that ruby! To become like the Proverbs 31 woman, we must humble ourselves and see our flaws. We must be willing to change some things: our attitudes, our thought patterns, our work ethic, our words, and what we spend our time on. But by God's grace, you can become a woman of noble character. Let's begin today.

WORK WITH EAGER HANDS

She seeks wool and flax, and works with willing hands.

—PROVERBS 31:13

When you roll out of bed in the morning, are you eagerly willing to do your daily chores? The Proverbs 31 woman oozes energy, industry, eagerness, and diligence. Are your hands willing and eager to get to work today?

I love how the Proverbs 31 woman's love for God overflows onto her family through her desire to serve them.

I was a recipient of willing hands when my family helped us move into our new home. What a blessing it was to see everyone working so hard. We even had some laughs at our one eager beaver (my oldest sister) who commanded my other sister and me to "push harder" while we scrubbed cabinets. Our insecurities at our lack of eagerness led us to hide in an upstairs bathroom where we could clean in a more carefree manner, but it was not long before she arrived to inspect our bathroom work and to give us more tips on how we could work more effectively and efficiently. Though we laughed then, afterward my husband and I were talking about how amazing her eagerness is. I want that! She is definitely a role model and inspiration to me in this area.

How Do We Get the Eagerness of the Proverbs 31 Woman?

1. *Pray.* Ask God to give you a willing attitude all day long.
2. *Do your work as unto the Lord.* Colossians 3:23 says, "Whatever you do, work heartily, as for the Lord and not for men."
3. *Change your perspective.* Remember that each mundane chore you complete for your family is a labor of love. As you shop, cook dinner, fold the laundry, and clean out sinks, remember that these small tasks create a well-nurtured home and family.
4. *Research and find inspiration.* Read a book on how to be a better homemaker, and implement the author's techniques. Find a woman you know who has eager hands, and learn from her.
5. *Rest.* If you work all day with eager hands, you will feel exhausted. Do not let your need for rest discourage you. If all day long you have been feeding and caring for your family, you will be tired. God never condemns rest. He condemns laziness.

Do you have a Titus 2 role model? Invest some time in learning the skills of homemaking. And take some time today to pray, change your perspective, work with eager hands, and then rest. Your hands will be a blessing to all those who enter your sweet home.

SHOP TO THE GLORY OF GOD

She is like the ships of the merchant;
she brings her food from afar.

—PROVERBS 31:14

In verse 14, the Proverbs 31 woman is compared to merchant ships. What was a merchant ship? It was a ship that brought in all different kinds of cargo to the port. It would have included dyes, fabrics, spices, oils, food, and pottery.

The Proverbs 31 woman did not have a refrigerator, so she would have had to travel to the market daily, and sometimes she would have to go a long way to get all the things she needed for the day. She was willing to go the distance because of her love and care for her husband and children.

If someone were describing your style of shopping, how would she describe you? Are you like "the merchant ships"? Are you willing to go to great effort to find the best, most cost-effective, and healthiest ingredients for your family? Do you work hard at your shopping? Are you more into convenience foods, or are you willing to cook from scratch? Do you take special care to get a good price on your goods, or do you stop at the nearest corner store and just get something quick?

Let me say for the record: shopping is hard work (especially with little ones in tow). I know how much planning, time, and energy goes into it. If we are going to be like the Proverbs 31 woman, though, we have to be willing to turn mundane shopping into a creative expression of love for our families.

I must admit that while I love deals and am willing to go to a few different stores for them, I am not the best at couponing. I cook nearly every meal in the home but rarely completely from scratch. Most of my recipes are simple. I have a couple of close friends who cook everything from scratch—from homemade bread to homemade sauces, salad dressings, and desserts. I admire their willingness to work hard in the kitchen.

Feeding our family fulfills a basic need. It's necessary. Are we doing it to the glory of God? Or are we too tired to cook the family a good meal? Strive to excel in meeting this basic need for your family. And shop to the glory of God!

RISE EARLY

She rises while it is yet night and provides food for her household and portions for her maidens.

—PROVERBS 31:15

The Proverbs 31 woman rises early to provide food for her family and to provide portions for her servant girls.

The word "portions" in this passage actually means work. She rises early to feed her family and delegate the day's work that needs to be done. You may insist, "I don't have servants!" My sentiments exactly! But let me suggest that your washing machine, dryer, dishwasher, and vacuum are just a few modern-day "servants" that lighten our workload tremendously compared to biblical times.

What are some benefits to rising early?

1. *Time with God.*
2. *Time alone for planning.* The Proverbs 31 woman delegated the day's work. She knew what needed to be done, and she owned her role as the manager of her home. I like to use the morning quietness to think clearly and write a list of what I need to get done that day.

3. *Time for making breakfast, packing lunches, and even some dinner preps.* The priority of providing food for her family got the Proverbs 31 woman out of bed in the morning!
4. *Time for family devotions.* If your family is all home at that time, it may be a good time to read God's Word together.

HOW TO DISCIPLINE YOURSELF TO RISE EARLY

1. Determine what time you plan to rise, and make it the same six days a week.
2. Get to bed early—at least seven hours before your wake time.
3. Pray and ask God to help you rise early.
4. Get up!

If you are in a season of life where you are nursing a baby or caring for a sick family member, please do not let this put guilt on you. There are seasons of life when we are not able to rise early. God never commands that we do. Rather, we see the example of the Proverbs 31 woman as a goal to attain.

If mornings are hectic and chaotic in your home, you can change that by rising earlier. Rising early can change the entire course of your day and will bless your family.

DO YOU HAVE A DREAM?

She considers a field and buys it; out of her earnings she plants a vineyard.

—PROVERBS 31:16 NIV

In verse 16, we see the work ethic of the Proverbs 31 woman.

First, *she considers a field*. She is not rash to jump into things. She is patient, cautious, and prayerful. She sees a field and can imagine what it could become. She is a visionary! I love that about her. She is creative.

Second, *she buys the field*. No matter how you translate it, this is a business deal. The Proverbs 31 woman went outside of her home and worked. She buys the field. Rather than spending the family's extra money on frivolous pleasures for herself, she wisely invests in something that will benefit the family.

Third, *she plants a vineyard*. Planting a vineyard is not an easy task. But she works hard, and as a result, her family benefits! At harvesttime they will have plentiful fruit and drink.

Do you have a dream? Do you have a talent you wish you could use to contribute to your family's finances? Follow the Proverbs 31 woman's plan.

Consider

Take time to pray about your dream. Ask God if this is the right season of life to invest time and money into this dream. Will this pull you away from your family or benefit your family?

Buy

Most likely resources will be necessary for your dream to take place. You may have to buy materials, renovate a room in your home, or purchase new clothing. Whatever it is, be wise. Be prudent with your family's money.

Plant

Here's where the rubber meets the road. You must work hard to accomplish your dream. It won't happen overnight. It will take day in, day out oversight and care. There'll be setbacks and frustrations. You must persevere to reap the fruit of your labor.

I experienced this verse when I considered starting the blog at WomenLivingWell.org. In 2008, it was just a dream. For nine months I considered the dream and prayed, "Should I or should I not start a website?" Was this some silly idea I was coming up with, or was this a work God wanted me to do? I consulted my husband, and together we considered the time factor. *Do I have the time? Is this the right season of life? What is my purpose?* One big benefit was that I could do a blogging ministry from home, unlike the ministry I was doing at the time.

We knew I had the passion, but time is a commodity that we value highly. Could I really squeeze it in and still accomplish our other family goals? Together my husband and I decided yes, this was a dream placed in my heart from God.

Once I had considered the dream and the time factor, it was time to buy. I purchased the domain Womenlivingwell.org, a blog design, and a few other items.

Now I am in the planting part. Daily I have to work to see the dream take shape. Every woman, no matter what her profession, has a dream in her heart. We all have common dreams placed in our hearts by God—to be the best wives, moms, and homemakers we can be. But after that we each have unique talents and gifts. When the talent and timing match the dream (and your husband is in full support, which you will find out during the "consideration" time), I believe God is in it.

Right now in this season of life, it may not be the time to invest time or finances in your dream, or maybe right now your family is in a place financially where you must work outside the home full-time. The dream job may not be available to you, but you must work to meet your family's needs. I have received e-mails from blog readers who long to be home, but this will never be a reality because of their circumstances. God sees you and knows your every need. He is pleased with your diligent heart that is willing to work hard for your family. If you work full-time, this means your life will be a bit fuller . . . you will have to be a good manager of your time to keep up with your home life. Your husband and children will need to chip in with housework, and while your children are young, you will need to say a strong no to many opportunities that come your way for fun or ministry. These nos are only a sacrifice for a season. I have found this comforting on days when I must say no to fun or ministry opportunities because of homeschooling. The children will eventually grow up, and this guard on our time will expand to include the things we wish we could do right now, but whatever work God has called you to today, do it like the Proverbs 31 woman . . . to the glory of God!

P.S. YOUR HANDS ARE BEAUTIFUL

*She opens her hand to the poor and reaches
out her hands to the needy.*

—PROVERBS 31:20

In Proverbs 31:20, a physical feature of this beautiful woman is mentioned for the first time—her hands. Up until now, her hands have been furiously working, sewing, planting, cooking, and shopping, and here they take center stage as she reaches out to those outside of her home.

Look down and examine your hands. Are they young or old? Soft or calloused? Sun spotted? Do your veins show? Do you think your hands are beautiful? Often our hands are one of the first places to show our age. They have worked hard serving our husbands, children, and the needy. What a blessing it is to have two hands!

My sister Jennifer once shared this story with me:

"P.S. Your hands are beautiful." This was what my in-laws wrote inside my birthday card at the end of their very nice note to me.

A few weeks before my birthday, I was at a family get-together, and something came up about "hands." I'm not sure how exactly the conversation went, but I know that I made the comment that the one place I have started to see my body aging is in my hands.

When I look down at them, which I realized is frequently during the day, they have begun to look different, older to me.

My mother-in-law said that the one thing she remembered about her own mother was her beautiful hands. I remembered her sharing about this before, and I believe that she meant more than just the outside beauty of beautiful skin with perfectly groomed nails. Those who had the privilege of knowing her mother, Louise, know that her life was one of active service to our Lord and that she did have beautiful hands because they did beautiful things for His glory.

When I read my birthday card with the message, "P.S. Your hands are beautiful," the full meaning of that small statement touched me.

It reminded me of what Paul said to the church at Thessalonica. First Thessalonians 4:11–12 says, "Aspire to live quietly, and to mind your own affairs, and to work with your hands, as we instructed you, so that you may walk properly before outsiders and be dependent on no one."

These verses should cause us to look at the work that we do as women and ask ourselves:

- Am I leading a quiet life?
- Am I minding my own business, the tasks that God has called me to do?
- Am I working faithfully with my hands in my daily life as an act of worship to my Lord?
- Is my work winning the respect of outsiders?
- Am I bringing glory to my Lord with the works of my hands?
- Would God think my hands are beautiful?

Dear reader, do not be discouraged as you toil day in and day out for loved ones. When we use our hands for God's glory, He is pleased.

Examine your hands with a new perspective. Do not judge the beauty of your hands by the outside, but rather by the lives they have touched.

PITY OR PRAISE?

*Give her of the fruit of her hands, and let
her works praise her in the gates.*

—PROVERBS 31:31

We have seen diligence in every aspect of the Proverbs 31 woman's life as she cares for her husband, children, servants, and even the poor. She rises early, stays up late, plants a vineyard, and sews her own clothes, her family's clothing, the tapestries, and beddings! In the end, what does she get for all of her hard labor? A prize, trophy, or plaque? No; she receives the praise of those around her, declaring indeed she is rare.

Let's reflect for a moment on the above list. Do you think she wanted to be pitied for the lowly work she had to do? Do you think she moped around imagining that the grass was greener for the lady down the road? She had to wake so early to care for her loved ones. She had to work so late at night to get all of the sewing work done. She had to be exhausted! Should we pity the Proverbs 31 woman?

I mean, where are the spa days? DisneyLand vacations? The raise with the corner office and bonus checks? Proverbs 31:28 says, "Her children rise up and call her blessed; her husband also, and he praises her." Her reward is the praise of her closest loved ones. And so we must ask:

1. What do your children think of you?
2. What does your husband think of you?

Some may say, "Praise is not much of a reward." But truly, how many wives do you know who long for their husbands' appreciation and acknowledgment of what they do? How many parents do you see struggling with teens who are unappreciative or even rebellious? The Proverbs 31 woman does not face these struggles. Wouldn't you take the peace, love, and harmony of a peaceful home over a free family vacation filled with strife?

Let's switch gears. I have been known to say, "Who you are at home is who you really are." But I want to add, you cannot be warm to those inside your home and cold to those outside your home and be like the Proverbs 31 woman.

Her character was clearly seen by those outside her home also. Verse 31 says, "Let her works praise her in the gates." Not only do those inside her home praise her, but now we see her being praised by those outside her home! Double bonus!

So, at the end of the day, do we pity or praise the Proverbs 31 woman?

To me, life is empty without the people in my life. And though I never want to selfishly seek praise from others, we see that it is the natural outcome of a woman who lives her life poured out for her family and friends.

Does God pity or praise the Proverbs 31 woman? He praises her. It is God we ultimately desire to please. And though this world may be confused by our dreams, visions, and goals, one day when we stand before God's throne, it will all be clear.

Proverbs 31:10 says, "An excellent wife who can find? She is far more precious than jewels." Indeed, sweet Christian sister, you are rare, and your worth is beyond any earthly treasure. Now go treasure the people in your life, and pursue pleasing God. Walk with the King!

Conclusion

WHAT IS YOUR DRIVING FORCE?

*God thunders wondrously with his voice; he does
great things that we cannot comprehend.*

—JOB 37:5

When I was a child, my mom would wrap her big, fuzzy green robe around herself, give us our packed lunches, and kiss us good-bye in the mornings. She always stood at the front window and watched as we got onto the bus. There was never a time I looked back and she was not there in the window with her eyes on us. And when we returned from school, my mom was there waiting for us with a snack and a listening ear. Mom always had her Bible on the kitchen table—evidence that she had been studying her Bible while we were in school. Just as my mother daily served physical food for me and my sisters, she also served us spiritual food. She always had a verse on the tip of her tongue for every situation I was facing. By the world's standards, my mom was not a successful woman. She didn't have a college degree or a corner office, but she pursued holiness tenaciously! Holiness was her driving force.

As I mentioned earlier, we have a glorious oak tree in our front yard. It stands tall and proud all winter long, catching the snow on its branches. Then come spring, its blossoms bring us joy. Each summer we soak up the shade it brings us, and in the fall, it puts on a fireworks display of autumn colors. I can't see the roots, but clearly they go deep. How deep are your roots?

It is in the secret discipline of private prayer and meditation on God's Word that our roots grow deep into the rich soil of holiness.

But the reality is . . . *holiness has never been the driving force of the majority.*

We live in a culture where prayerless tweets and status updates fly through our fingers without a thought toward holiness. The lines between principle and impulse have been blurred as information rapidly swirls like wind about us, moving us one direction and then the next.

All the information of every library in the world, we carry in our purses in the form of our iPhones. But most of the food for our minds found there is emptiness; emptiness served on a platter for our starved souls to feed on.

Nineteenth-century preacher Charles Spurgeon once said, "All the libraries and studies are mere emptiness compared with our closets."[1] What is the closet Spurgeon speaks of? His private prayer closet. It may be cliché, but it is also true: prayer changes things. The depth of our private prayer will determine the depth of our holiness.

First Peter 1:16 reminds us, "It is written, 'You shall be holy, for I am holy.'" Our standard of holiness does not come from culture or the relativism of our modern age; our standard of holiness is absolute—it is God's holiness.

The world tells a man who seeks holiness that he is "hung up, not in touch with his feelings, a do-gooder, a party pooper, holier-than-thou—any label that will exonerate the rest of us of the responsibility of being Christlike. We pity his naïveté, his narrowness, his unreality, never suspecting that there could be in our midst a few whose minds are set on things above because their lives are hid with Christ."[2]

If our roots are not deep into the rich soil of God's Word, we will be swayed by the empty soul food we feed on. If holiness is not our driving force, we will be blown to and fro by the ways of the world and the emotions of our hearts. Remember, holiness has never been the driving force of the majority.

And so I'm reminded of the daily consistency of my mother's prayers and study of the Bible. I'm reminded of her faithfulness to carry God's Word in her heart and on her tongue. I'm reminded of her clear discernment of which worldly philosophies or feelings to reject. And I'm reminded of her tenacity for holiness. And it all began with a Bible in the kitchen—a mother's prayer closet.

The Road Map to Living Well

My mom wasn't perfect. I am not perfect. None of us has arrived. We all are on our journey toward living well. And every journey needs a trusted road map. So, I want to encourage you to pause for a moment and evaluate:

Evaluate Your Walk with God

Are you daily spending time in God's Word and prayer? How can you improve your walk with God?

Suggestion: Ponder your schedule, and then write down a set time for quiet each day. Mine is 6:30 every morning. Consider starting or joining a Good Morning Girls group. I e-mail my girls every morning Monday through Friday. Enrollment for new sessions begins every three months online.

Evaluate Your Marriage

What is one word you'd use to describe your marriage? *Easy, frustrating, growing, romantic, hard, strong, amazing?* What is one thing you know your husband wishes you'd change in your life?

Suggestion: Write down the steps you can take to change that area in your life. For example: being more organized, cooking healthier, being more flexible, being more respectful, kissing him like you mean it more often . . .

Evaluate Your Children

What was a high point and a low point for each of your children this past year? What is one thing that each of your children need from you right now?

Suggestion: Write down the steps you can take toward giving your children what they need. For example: reading to them more, one-on-one time, your undivided attention, memorizing God's Word together, manners training . . .

Evaluate Your Homemaking

What areas in your home need your attention right now? Is there something you could commit to accomplishing this month that would bless your family?

Suggestion: Start with the simple things, like lighting a candle, turning on soft music, and putting something homemade in the oven. Work on the atmosphere of your home and heart.

Choose a Theme Word for the Year

Pause and look over your evaluation. Now choose a theme word for the year. Some words I have claimed in the past are *peace, discipline, joy,* and right now I'm *simplifying.*

I want to *simplify* many areas of my life so I have more space to pray, laugh, tickle, write, listen, create, rest, hug, read, connect, and love more deeply than I've ever loved. In my pursuit for peace in my home and in my heart, I have found that there are some things in my life that need to be simplified in order to create space for peace—so essentially, I'm pursuing peace through simplifying.

FROM LOOKING OUT TO LOOKING AHEAD

Three years have passed since the day I stood in that hotel room on the thirty-seventh floor looking out over Manhattan, about to go on the air with Rachael Ray. This girl who begged God long ago while living in Chicago to be used by God was realizing a dream. But this was not the peak of my life. The peak will be when I close my eyes and cross over to the shores of heaven and walk with my King on the streets of gold. It is with faith that I say that greater things are yet to come.

Today, back in my home, my Bible sits on my kitchen table. As a woman, I am feverishly trying to follow in my mother's footsteps, but I struggle to hear God's voice in the midst of a noisy world. Each morning I fight with my blankets to rise early and meet with God. Then I wrestle the voices of social media calling out my name to greet me and chat awhile. But victory is found as I open God's Word and gulp down a huge glass of living water.

"Not that I have already obtained this or am already perfect, but I press on to make it my own, because Christ Jesus has made me his own. Brothers [and sisters!], I do not consider that I have made it my own. But one thing I do: forgetting what lies behind and straining forward to what lies ahead, I press on toward the goal for the prize of the upward call of God in Christ Jesus" (Phil. 3:12–14).

We haven't arrived. We must press on. A woman's journey here on earth can be uncertain, and the road can be rocky. If we desire to be women who live well, we must daily run to the living well and drink from it. Holiness must be our driving force. Together, let's intentionally tune out the clamor of the world as we listen to the voice of the Creator of this world. He loves you so!

Keep walking with the King!

NOTES

Chapter 2: No Time for a Quiet Time

1. Good Morning Girls, http://www.goodmorninggirls.org /gmg-online-bible-studies.
2. Elizabeth George, *Life Management for Busy Women* (Eugene, OR: Harvest House, 2002), 27.

Chapter 3: How Thirsty Am I?

1. Edith Schaeffer, *The Hidden Art of Homemaking* (Carol Stream, IL: Tyndale, 1971), 145.
2. Edward W. Goodrick and John R. Kohlenberger III, *The NIV Exhaustive Concordance* (Grand Rapids, MI: Zondervan, 1990), 67.
3. Ibid., 233.
4. John Piper, *A Hunger for God* (Wheaton, IL: Crossway, 1997), 20.
5. *Merriam-Webster's 11th Collegiate Dictionary*, s.v. "pacify," http://www.merriam-webster.com/dictionary /pacifies?show=0&t=1347334486.
6. Dictionary.com, s.v. "satisfied," http://dictionary.reference.com /browse/satisfied.

Chapter 4: The Effects of the Media Revolution

1. Elisabeth Elliot, *Discipline* (Grand Rapids, MI: Revell, 1982), 54.

Chapter 5: Never Walk Alone

1. Janet Thompson, *Woman to Woman Mentoring* (Nashville, TN: LifeWay Christian Resources, 2000).

Chapter 6: The Time-Warp Wife

1. Edward W. Goodrick and John R. Kohlenberger III, *The NIV Exhaustive Concordance* (Grand Rapids, MI: Zondervan, 1990), 951, 1804.
2. Emerson Eggerichs, *Love and Respect* (Nashville: Integrity, 2004), 4.
3. Karen Ehman, *LET. IT. GO. How to Stop Running the Show and Start Walking in Faith* (Grand Rapids, MI: Zondervan, 2012), 71.

Chapter 7: Marriage in the Age of Media

1. Kesavan Unnikrishnan, "Study: Facebook Cited in a Third of Divorces in 2011," *Digital Journal*, January 1, 2012.
2. Karen Ehman, *LET. IT. GO. How to Stop Running the Show and Start Walking in Faith* (Grand Rapids, MI: Zondervan, 2012), 191.
3. Gary Chapman, *Things I Wish I'd Known Before I Got Married* (Chicago: North Field Publishing, 2010), chap. 4.
4. Comment left on Women Living Well, http://womenlivingwell .org/2011/08/my-birthday-and-the-start-of-a-new-series.

Chapter 9: The "Completing Him" Marriage Challenge, Week 1

1. http://www.divorcestatistics.org/.
2. Stormie Omartian, *The Power of a Praying Wife* (Eastbourne, East Sussex, UK: Kingsway, 2001).

Chapter 10: The "Completing Him" Marriage Challenge, Week 2

1. John Piper, *This Momentary Marriage* (Wheaton, IL: Crossway, 2009), 24.
2. Dr. Gary Chapman, *The Five Love Languages* (Chicago: Northfield, 2009).

3. Paula Rinehart, *What's He Really Thinking?* (Nashville: Thomas Nelson, 2009), 95.

Chapter 11: The Influence of a Mother

1. Elisabeth Elliot, *Discipline* (Grand Rapids, MI: Revell, 1982), 89.

Chapter 14: I'm Gonna Blow My Top!

1. *Matthew Henry's Whole Bible Commentary*, Ecclesiastes 9:17; available at http://www.biblegateway.com/resources /matthew-henry/Eccl.9.13-Eccl.9.18.
2. Sally Clarkson, The Better Mom, "Weary Mama," December 6, 2011, http://www.thebettermom.com/2011/12/weary-mama/.

Chapter 15: Schools of Thought, Schools of Choice

1. http://www.christianhomeeducation.org/publicschools.html.

Chapter 17: Making Your Home a Haven

1. Edith Schaeffer, *The Hidden Art of Homemaking* (Carol Stream, IL: Tyndale, 1971), 40.
2. J. R. Miller, *The Family* (San Antonio: Vision Forum, 1882), 100.
3. Schaeffer, *The Hidden Art of Homemaking*, 119.
4. Ibid., 124

Chapter 19: Media and Your Homemaking—Times Have Changed!

1. Chris Brogan, "Don't Be Chris Brogan," *ChrisBrogan.com*, October 3, 2010, available at http://www.chrisbrogan.com /dont-be-chris-brogan/.

Conclusion: What Is Your Driving Force?

1. E. M. Bounds, *Power Through Prayer* (Lexington, KY: Trinity, 2012), 16.
2. Elisabeth Elliot, *Discipline* (Grand Rapids, MI: Revell, 1982), 60–61.

ACKNOWLEDGMENTS

To my tall, dark, and handsome husband, Keith—God gave me you! You told me ten years ago you believed one day I would write a book. I laughed. No way did I ever in my wildest dreams believe this would be happening—but here it is, honey! Without you, there'd be no book. Thank you for believing in me, supporting me, loving me, and having a vision. I love you always, forever and a day!

To Alex and Alexis—You are an inspiration. Your morning hugs and sunshine smiles make my mommy heart burst with joy. Alex, you are my favorite little boy in the whole world. Alexis, you are my favorite little girl in the whole world. You are irreplaceable, forever loved, and covered in prayers by your mommy.

To Dad and Mom—Thank you for planning wonderfully inviting times for my children so I could get away and write this book. Your help, prayers, and listening ears, along this writing journey, have been priceless. Thank you for letting me spill your life out all over these pages for the world to see.

To Kristen and Jennifer—I am so blessed to walk in the shadow of my two big sisters. You have taught me so much about serving God, marriage, parenting, homemaking, and more. Thank you for putting up with your little sister's passion and letting me splatter your pictures all over Facebook! You are good sports! I love you both!

To the sweetest Grandma ever—You are the living, breathing Proverbs 31 and Titus 2 woman. Thank you for your heart that so willingly and diligently serves your family. I will always treasure your unconditional love and security you have given me. I love you.

To Angela Perritt—My best friend for more than twenty years and fearless leader of GoodMorningGirls.org. Your tender words give me courage to write. Without you there'd be no YouTubes. You were the one who gave me confidence when I had none. Your prayers and long pep talks on the phone have kept me going when I've been ready to throw in the towel. You are beautiful inside and out, and I treasure your friendship.

To the five original Good Morning Girls—Thank you for a fantastic two years! I will forever hold dear in my heart our morning e-mails, prayers, support, laughter, tears, playdates, and book clubs in our backyards. I love you girls! Thank you, Kelly, for helping us choose the name "Good Morning Girls," and thank you, Aimee, for coining the phrase "Walk with the King." Look how God has multiplied our five loaves and two fishes!

To my current Good Morning Girls group—Janelle, Kelly, Kimmy, Kristy, Kara, Aimee, and Becky, thank you for the accountability, prayers, and listening ears. Your spiritual roots run deep, and you both challenge and inspire me to keep pressing on every day. Thank you for always being just a click away!

To my soul sisters—Angela, Clare, Janelle, Darlene, Joy, and Ruth, you are stellar women of faith! Your writing blesses me every day. I can't believe how closely God has knit our hearts together through our passion to write. I am honored to serve alongside you all online. Keep writing and keep shining!

To Nicki—Thank you for sharing your cleaning schedule with me!

To Whitney—You have been a huge blessing to me and Ang!

Thank you for always having a willing heart to serve the GMG community!

To Jennifer and Joe Thorn—I am so excited to have my college roomie along on this online writing journey! Jen, your writing is awesome! And to Joe—our discussions for years over the dinner table in college forever changed me spiritually. Thank you for making me wrestle with my beliefs and learn how to know and love God more deeply.

To Karen Ehman—Words cannot express how grateful I am for you! The first time we talked on the phone, I knew I had a forever friend! I admire you and have so much more to learn from you. Thank you for letting me bounce the words of this book off of you. You are a gem!

To Esther Fedorkevich, my agent—Thank you for taking a chance on this first-time author. I am so thankful for you and can't wait to see what's next . . .

To the "Women Living Well" blog readers—Oh, friends, I never in a million years dreamt that anyone would actually read what I write. But you do, and you keep coming back and graciously encouraging me and sharing your hearts. I have so far to go on this journey and thank you for joining me on it. I can't wait to see how God is going to work in your life! Keep walking with the King!

Now to him who is able to keep you from stumbling
and to present you blameless before the presence of his
glory with great joy, to the only God, our Savior, through
Jesus Christ our Lord, be glory, majesty, dominion, and
authority, before all time and now and forever. Amen.

—JUDE vv. 24–25

INDEX

INDEX

ABOUT THE AUTHOR

Courtney Joseph has been married to her high school sweetheart for over sixteen years and classically educates her son and daughter at home. Courtney is a graduate of the Moody Bible Institute with a degree in Evangelism and Discipleship. After over a decade of leading women's Bible studies, mentorships, and workshops in her local church, she decided to move her ministry online at *WomenLivingWell.org* and *WomenLivingWell.TV.*

Courtney's passion and sincerity have made her a leader in the Christian blogging community. She has been featured on the nationally syndicated television program, *The Rachael Ray Show*, and has spoken at many national conferences including Relevant, Allume, She Speaks, The Nines, and Mom Heart.

Courtney's desire is to *see women living well* through discipleship in God's Word. This led her to cofound the rapidly growing, online Bible study community at *GoodMorningGirls.org*. There, thousands of women, globally, join together daily to dig into their Bibles through online devotionals, videos, free Bible reading plans, and tech-based accountability groups.

You can follow Courtney's ministry on Facebook, Twitter, Pinterest, and Instagram under the Profile: *Women Living Well*. Join her, as you walk with the King.